Jules Hoche, Charles R. Rogers

The Real Bismarck

Jules Hoche, Charles R. Rogers
The Real Bismarck
ISBN/EAN: 9783337383749

Printed in Europe, USA, Canada, Australia, Japan

Cover: Foto ©ninafisch / pixelio.de

More available books at **www.hansebooks.com**

THE
REAL BISMARCK

BY

JULES HOCHE

ILLUSTRATED

ENGLISHED BY
Mrs. CHARLES R. ROGERS

NEW YORK
R. F. FENNO & COMPANY, Publishers
9 AND 11 EAST SIXTEENTH STREET
1898

PREFACE.

Many qualities are essential to the biographer who is to successfully discharge the duties and responsibilities of his office. Of the first importance is impartiality; that is, an absence of all preconceived prejudice against the man whose portrait is to be drawn. Honesty also is indispensable—the honesty of the mirror, and of a mirror sufficiently correct not to send back to an ape which should chance to regard himself therein, the reflection of an apostle—or the reverse.

Before and above all must the biographer furnish his readers with the psychological key to the actions of his hero (I was about to say his patient); a sketch explanatory of his moral nature, a skeleton as exact in outline, as luminous as that of an opaque body traversed by the Roentgen rays. For the words and deeds of a man, however famous he may be, interest us only commensurately with our ability to divine their motive and purpose; and proportionately with the manner, more or less complicated, in which they explain, reflect, commentate the mysterious depths and shallows of his soul.

In a word it is necessary that the human type posing before us, the being of flesh and bone, clothed, armed with defiance, intrenched behind the sympathy or hate with which he has been able to inspire his contemporaries—shall become suddenly fluid, incorporeal, reduced to a simple psycho-physical expression; a mental equation of one or several volumes, the solution of which the reader has the right to exact from the first page.

If the application of this theory be an essential of all biography of any seriousness, it becomes indispensable to that of a man like Bismarck, of whom his enigmatical personality invited as many detractors as admirers, and of whom has been spoken at the same time so much both of good and evil that it is impossible to form an opinion concerning him if one be not in possession of the psychological key to which I have alluded.

So, contrary to the usage of those writers who, before an undertaking similar to this, have begun by deprecating their incompetency for the task, I believe I may assert that my readers will find in this study the two essential elements which are lacking in all other biographies of Bismarck: namely, absolute impartiality and an exact psychological theory, solving in the most simple, lucid and conclusive manner the vital problem offered to the entire world by the unobtrusive personage who, during a half-century directed, more or less officially, the destiny of a great part of Europe.

I was quite small when for the first time the name of Bismarck was revealed to me by iron and fire ("ferro et igne" according to the good Bismarckian formula) and by the conversation of my elders, some of whom, alas! paid the tribute of one or two members to that iron and fire which then rained upon besieged Strasbourg; still more particularly was it made known to me by the bursting shells which all day long filled the neighborhood about our house with a music so sweet to my childish ears that I resisted the impulse to associate the name of Bismarck, the indirect cause of the music, with those of Croquemitaine, Troppmann, Mephistopheles, who, with the occult Master of the invading Germans, shared the execrations of the besieged.

Shortly after, I found myself in the situation of the perplexed man whom an old allegorical print represents nude between two garments—one made in the style of yesterday, the other in that of to-morrow. Thanks to the treaty of Frankfort, I had all the trouble in the world to retain the garment of yesterday—that which the law of might attempted to wrest from me. The remembrance of my nudity for a long time pursued me, imbuing me with a profound scepticism regarding certain high-flown phrases which form some good patriots' stock-in-trade of eloquence.

Never for an instant, however, did the ridiculous idea present itself, that a single man, even Bismarck himself, could be the sole cause of the accumulating distress of my country; I preferred to see in this distress only a phenomenon which was an inevitable result of the social and political evolution of Europe.

Hence my impartial attitude toward the man who has played so distinguished a part in the fatal events which were the cause of my being withdrawn from an ethnical family hearth to which I have never since sought to return.

These facts noted, I plunge without further preamble into the psychological sketch which I have promised the reader.

From an exclusively biological view-point Bismarck is undeniably a natural force; which explains in a general way the inequalities, the exaggerations, the contradictions, the bewildering contrasts which seemed to characterize his political life. Yet this does not explain his more intimate and familiar personality, so chameleon-like in its charm that public appreciation of it has varied as frequently as it has found writers to describe it; while a single word, a simple epithet coupled with his name would have sufficed to banish all uncertainty and render the obscurity luminous.

Bismarck is above all else a humorist.

Into politics and diplomacy he carried the same gestures, the same attitudes which, in literature, distinguish Sterne, Carlyle, Lamb, Heine, even Schopenhauer; he borrows from this one and that his malice, his artful joviality, from the others their love of antithesis, their comical conceits; from all, their paradoxical spirit, their disdain of others and of themselves, engrafted upon a brutal candour bordering upon cynicism; a cynicism in him hardly softened by extreme sensitiveness and a number of remarkable domestic virtues in which his monstrous egoism has been reabsorbed.

As a diplomatist he proclaimed the emptiness and vanity of all diplomacy; as a political orator he defended himself only by outbursts of whimsical humour and more or less witty sarcasms; further, while working zealously for God and the Fatherland, this Protestant patriot confesses his pessimism and the inanition of his faith. These tendencies, wholly characteristic of his humoristic temperament, are most frequently revealed in his speeches and in his unofficial correspondence. I will cite some examples; first, this passage in a letter addressed to Madame Bismarck, from Frankfort, where he was attending the federal Diet.

Unless external complications arise—and we federal delegates are as utterly incapable of producing them as of extricating ourselves from them—I know precisely what we shall do in one, two or five years; I would undertake to accomplish it in twenty-four hours if the others would be sensible and sincere a single day. I never doubted that these gentlemen had their food prepared in the most economical manner, yet such a total absence of rich ingredients confounds me, I admit. Send me your school-master or your road-surveyor and if they be washed and combed they will make as good diplomats as these. I am making prodigious progress in the art of saying nothing in an infinite number of words. I write letters of several pages, with perfect clearness and precision; and if, after having read them, Manteuffel is able to tell me what they are about, he knows more than I. None, not even the most worthless Democrat, can conceive the emptiness and charlatanism of diplomacy.

Humour, according to his own definition, expresses itself by an impassability, an emotion rather concentrated than expansive; an emotion compounded of selfishness and sadness because it springs from the most profound depths of the being, and possessing an accidental character of hereditary physical instincts and affinities strongly dominating individual psychic tendencies. This last peculiarity has made of the gigantic Prussian, so pre-eminently organized for intellectual emancipation, a believer sad, resigned, bent under the double yoke of his God and of his Emperor, whose prerogatives he readily confounds; he is attached to this tyrannical duality as a dog to his master; yes, like one of those big dogs by which he loves to be surrounded, and some of which curiously resemble himself in their cold, steady gaze, their heavy eyebrows, the immobility of their leonine features, the rigidity of their powerful jaws.

One evening Bismarck explained to his guests at Ferrières in what manner his piety, in some sort atavic, I was about to say congenital, served as substratum to his political conscience and to all his aspirations which, be it said in passing, are at least a century behind the general evolution of the human mind:

I cannot comprehend how one may live without a belief in God and in a future life. Were not I a Christian I should not for an instant consent to remain at my post; did not I obey my God, did not I rely upon him I certainly should not concern myself with this world's grandeur. I have enough to live upon and a sufficiently distinguished position; why should I labour and torment myself ceaselessly? why expose myself to care, fatigue, calumny, did not I feel obliged to fulfil my duty toward God? Did not I believe in the divine will which has decreed that the German nation shall become great and virtuous, I should never have entered upon a political career or at least I should promptly renounce it. I do not know whence would come the sentiment of duty if not from God. Titles and decorations have no charm for me. I firmly believe in a future life, therefore I am a royalist! naturally I should incline to republicanism. It is to my unswerving faith alone that I owe the strength which has enabled me to resist all the absurdities imaginable for the past ten years. Deprive me of my faith and you despoil me of my country. Were not I a firm Christian, did not my edifice rest upon the miraculous base of religion, I should never have been the Chancellor whom you know. Find me a successor penetrated with the same principles and I will immediately retire. Ah, I should be glad to go! I adore the country, the woods—all nature enraptures me. Separate me from God and I pack my trunks to-morrow and go to cultivate my oats at Varzin

And now permit me to follow these two extracts, wherein the soul of the humorist Bismarck reveals itself in two essential aspects, with this definition of humour borrowed from a writer whom the ex-Chancellor much cultivated— M. Taine:

In the humorist the physical nature, hidden and oppressed under habits of melancholy reflection, is exposed for an instant. You see a grimace, a mischievous gesture, then a swift return to the habitual solemnity. Add to this the unexpected flashes of imagination. The humorist encloses a poet. Suddenly, in the monotonous twilight of prose, at the end of a lane of argument, a landscape sparkles; beautiful or ugly, it matters not which so that it be striking. These inequalities well express the German solitary, energetic, imaginative, cultivating violent contrasts founded upon sad personal reflection, with unexpected returns to physical instinct, so different from the Latin and classic races, races of artists and orators among whom all write in the public view, none is happy except in the contemplation of harmonious forms, in whom the imagination is disciplined and to whom sensuality seems natural.

It is easily observed that this definition from the "Histoire de la littérature anglaise" applies astonishingly well to the psychology of Bismarck, such as, deduced from his confidential correspondence and from his familiar conversation, it would appear that it should be. Furthermore, is not this the same man who uttered the disconcerting aphorism: " It is unnecessary to take anything seriously"? and whose public life seemed to be inspired by Schopenhauer's maxim: " Neither to love nor to hate is the first half of the science of life; to hold the tongue and to believe nothing, the second half."

Thus are accounted for his eternal contradictions, the constant tacking, the inexhaustible resource, the brusque destruction of the axis of his politics. For the opinion of some biographers who accord him above all a remarkable steadfastness of mind, is laughable to those who have studied more closely his political sayings and doings, his innumerable changes of side, so marvellously adapted to the incoherency of European diplomacy—incoherencies to which Bismarck but accommodates himself most cleverly, while seeming to direct them.

To those who proclaim and pompously praise his steadfastness of mind he would certainly be the first to reply in the mocking tone familiar with him, that steadfastness of purpose was an excellent quality for a grocer or any other tradesman, but that it would be the most objectionable ingredient to introduce into a parliamentary salad, the ragoûts of chancery, where it is the first essential to know how to metamorphose the errors of yesterday into the truths of to-morrow.

To those who insist upon treating him as a great political genius, a man of fate marked, like Richelieu and Napoleon, with the seal of a tragic predestination, Prince Bismarck would repeat what he one day said to Mr. Blowitz—that he does not believe in a great providential man; that according to his belief political celebrities owe their reputations, if not to hazard at least to circumstances which they themselves cannot have foreseen.

As a matter of fact the ex-Chancellor himself perhaps owes to a sally of superlative humour all his political fortune, or at least the unexpected course which his destiny took in 1839. He was then Referendary in the civil administration at Aix-la-Chapelle. One of his chiefs having kept him waiting a long time in the antechamber he gravely said, when at last he was introduced: "I came to converse with you, but upon reflection, instead I will hand in my resignation."

This absurd incident did indeed turn the young Bismarck from a bureaucratic career.

THE REAL BISMARCK.

I.

Ancestors of Otto von Bismarck—The Goblet of the Old Marshal—Schönhausen and His Two Châteaux—The Parents of Bismarck—An Interrupted Honeymoon—The French Invasion—The Tribulations of a Prussian Major of Cavalry—A Singular Birth-Announcement—The Vulnerability of a Stone Hercules—Birth of Malvina von Bismarck.

The genealogy of the ex-Chancellor, Otto von Bismarck, presents a long line of soldiers and troopers of Brandenbourg or Pomerania, of no particular interest to us. Their existence was passed in drinking, hunting and spilling their blood upon every battle-field in Prussia.

Augustus Frederic von Bismarck, the great-grandfather of the ex-Chancellor, was colonel of a regiment of dragoons and perished at Czaslau, in a battle fought against the Austrians (May, 1742). His wife, born von Dewitz, was descended in a direct line from the Brandenbourgian Marshal Derfflinger, one of whose nieces, Charlotte von Schoenfeldt, was married to the Chancellor's grandfather, Charles Alexander, second son of Colonel von Bismarck. Thus the descendants of Charles Alexander had in their veins the blood of the Derfflingers, and Bismarck, who respects his ancestors, has preserved a silver goblet ornamented with a medallion wrought in silver, of the old Marshal; a goblet in which has long been served the beer at the famous Parliamentary receptions at the Radziwill Palace.

Charles Alexander pursued peace and knowledge, but the warlike spirit of his forebears was revived in his four sons, and most irresistibly in the youngest, Charles William Ferdinand, the father of the Chancellor, who, at the age of twelve years was enrolled a carbineer of the Guard and in 1792 took part in the campaign against France, as one of the ordnance-officers of the Duke of Brunswick.

Of his ancestry, then, it is seen that Otto von Bismarck has somewhat to be proud. His early studies suffered much from his own turbulent and dissipated character; he was by no means the meditative, abstracted child which a celebrity is supposed to be in early life. Strong and healthy, energetic and overflowing with physical vigour, he never missed an occasion for slighting his school exercises. At the age of sixteen the preparation for his examinations was willingly neglected for his favourite sports, hunting, fishing and long excursions on horse-back.

Otto von Bismarck was born at Schönhausen in Brandenbourg on April 1, 1815.

The castle of Schönhausen, as represented in the engraving, dates from the eighteenth century; the period at which Colonel von Bismarck, Otto's great-grandfather, had it reconstructed upon the foundations of the ancient feudal castle. The father of Otto von Bismarck, having retired with the rank of major, was married to Louise Menken, a little *bourgeoise;* the granddaughter of a professor of philosophy and daughter of a King's councillor whose death had occurred in 1801. Of this marriage were born six children, of whom only three have survived: the ex-Chancellor (Otto), his brother Bernard and his sister Malvina, who was married in 1844 to Oscar von Arnim, a member of the Reichstag.

Bismarck has always been profoundly devoted to his sister Malvina, who will be frequently mentioned in this volume; to her are addressed the letters by turns sentimental, enthusiastic, mocking, which, better than any official document, form a kind of anthology of the habits of mind most characteristic of the ex-Chancellor.

Before going farther it may be as well to remark that the castle of Schönhausen here referred to is the old patrimonial estate of Bismarck, of much less importance than the great seigneurial castle situated in the same neighbourhood. This last belonged also to one of the branches of the Bismarck family, who found it necessary to sell it. We shall see somewhat later how the Chancellor possessed himself of the property and of the ennobling particle which belongs with the domain; for it is only by virtue of this particle that the Bismarck-Schönhausens have since been entitled to call themselves Bismarcks *von* Schönhausen.

In July, 1806, William Ferdinand, Otto's father, quitted the army, as has been said, to be married to Louise Menken. The two young people had met at Court, where Louise Menken, being an orphan, was especially petted. William Ferdinand took his wife to Schönhausen, but their honeymoon was clouded less than three months later by the sadness and alarm attendant upon the war. The French invaded the country about October 1st of the same year, and in a château near Schönhausen Marshal Soult established his head-quarters.

The Germans have not a little reproached us for the depredations committed by our troops during that invasion. Even at Schönhausen, they say, everything was ravaged by Soult's men. It might be supposed that the genealogical tree of the Bismarcks had been slashed with innumerable sabre-cuts; that even Madame von Bismarck had been in imminent peril of violation.

As a matter of fact the young couple received not the smallest injury.

Fear led them to seek refuge, one night, in a neighbouring

forest, and profound was their surprise, upon returning next day, to find the village and the château still unharmed. There had not been disturbed even a hiding-place in which Ferdinand von Bismarck had so clumsily concealed some gold that he afterward found a few pieces scattered upon the soil about the hole; none had taken the trouble to pick it up, and the whole treasure was discovered undisturbed. This circumstance, however, did not prevent the Prussian major from going the same day to the French general and asking for a guard of soldiers for picket duty; a favour which was immediately accorded. It is not, then, in the horrors of the invasion that the German Chancellor (who was not then born) finds a reason for his hatred of the French.

In 1816, one year after the birth of Otto, his parents inherited from a cousin the domains of Kültz, Kneiphof and Jarchelin; they established themselves upon the most considerable of the three, Kneiphof, situated in the district of Naugart, in Pomerania.

It is a singular coincidence that when Otto von Bismarck came into the world his mother determined to make of him later a diplomatist; as for his elder brother, Bernard, she decided that he should enter the civil administration. These two desires have been realized, contrary to the fate which generally overtakes such desires.

A circumstance which throws a peculiar light upon the customs of the German nobility of that time was the insertion in a local paper of the following announcement:

> The undersigned announces to his friends and acquaintances the happy deliverance of his wife of a well-conditioned boy, and excuses them from all felicitations.
>
> FERDINAND VON BISMARCK

The biographers of Bismarck have been at great pains to discover "remarkable characteristics" in the subject of their pens, even from the earliest years of his childhood. I have read and reread the anecdotes which have been offered, and I protest they have appeared to me so banal, so little significant, that I dare not risk their repetition here.

At the age of six years Otto was sent to join his brother Bernard at Plaman Institute in Berlin. The five or six years which were passed there have left him but regrettable memories. The food was insufficiently nourishing, the discipline severe, and despite the ascendency which the young Otto gained over his fellows, he was more feared by them than loved. Frequent vacations were happily a recompense for the tribulations there endured; when the small *pensionnaire* was permitted to renew his strength in the pure air of the woods and fields of Pomerania. He also profited by the opportunity to indulge to the full his precocious taste for the chase.

The following comical anecdote demonstrates the inadvisability of placing firearms in the hands of a youngster of eleven years; moreover, it is a revelation of the humorous temperament of Bismarck.

In a glade in the park at Schönhausen is a statue of Hercules, now half-covered with lichens. The little Otto returning one day from hunting and passing behind the mythological god, it occurred to him that it would be amusing to put a charge of lead into his legs.

His father, soon after discovering the misdeed, said to Otto: " Did you fire that shot? "

" Yes," replied the child, " but I didn't suppose he was so easily hurt. When I fired he put his right hand near the spot I hit and has not taken it away."

The Hercules is indeed represented with his right hand behind his back.

The elder Bismarck laughed at the child's droll idea and the incident was followed by no unpleasant consequences.

In 1827 was born the little Malvina, already mentioned, and Otto was entered at the Frederic-William grammar school, where, this time, he was so fortunate as to attract the notice of the distinguished professor, Dr. Bonnell, who was charmed by his frank, open face, his large eyes full of energy and intelligence. Under his direction the pupil Bismarck promptly distinguished himself, particularly in history and French. Otto himself became so attached to his master that, two years after, when his brother Bernard quitted the class in rhetoric, number one, in order to take up the study of the law—he followed Dr. Bonnell to the grammar-school of the *Cloître Gris*, and some months later became his pupil.

Notwithstanding Dr. Bonnell's praise (and how could he speak otherwise than in praise when the Chancellor so effectually proved his affection and gratitude for his old master, afterward director of the Werder grammar-school, as to confide to his care the education of his sons Herbert and William?), it cannot be said that Bismarck left a very brilliant record at the *Cloître Gris*. Not until April, 1832, did he succeed in passing the Baccalaureate, and his diploma shows a deplorable tendency to evade the course.

Charles-William Ferdinand von Bismarck, Father of the Chancellor.

II.

Bismarck at the University of Göttingen—The Handsome Student—Inaneness of Academical Vetoes—The Ulm Dogs Come Upon the Scene—First Conflict With the Rector—The Door of the Dungeon—The *Hannovera*—*A propos* of Boots—Bismarck Loses a Wager Relative to the Unification of Germany—The Duellist Interdicted by the Academic Council—Tardy Remorse—Bismarck is Expelled from Jena—Therapeutic Pork-Butcher's Meats—All's Well That Ends Well—Bismarck is Appointed *Auscultator*.

One month later, Otto von Bismarck became a law-student at the University of Göttingen. He was then a very pretty boy with curling hair, and " eyes clear and profound, which alone were expressive in the mask of immobility which his face wore, and which seemed to absorb all that they looked upon."

The impassive expression of his face is inherited, it appears, and all the vivacity of the mind, all the intensity of thought and volition takes refuge in the eyes; eyes of a remarkable depth and earnestness of expression! Already, also, was to be observed the same harmony of outline which later distinguished the face of the Imperial Chancellor; a face notable for its bilateral symmetry, for the breadth of brow, the clean-cut nose with its finely curved nostrils, the square, powerful chin, the dome-like shape of the head, the face, in short, of a Titan, which engravings and caricatures have sufficiently popularized to make further description unnecessary. The reader may, indeed, refer to the authentic portraits contained in this volume, which represent him at various ages.

A rapid growth had, at this period, almost spiritualized the student's features; his professors have since described him as a young man who too rapidly attained his growth and who was peculiarly tall and gaunt. The student-life of Otto von Bismarck was much like that of others of his kind, a life of drinking and fighting which leaves scant opportunity for study and which, in his case, came very near to compromising his entry upon the career which he had in view. Not that this dissipated existence was particularly to the taste of Otto von Bismarck; on the contrary, he had even then a devout love of nature, of the country, of great hunts; and his love of animals was so deeply rooted that he might perhaps have preferred the society of his dogs, which had become his inseparable companions, to that of his comrades in debauchery. Yet was not it necessary to make some sacrifice to win the honour of being admitted to a university which was then enjoying a European celebrity?

The habits of the German student have frequently been described. It is known that he has always a pipe or a chop in his mouth and that all quarrels are settled by duels with the rapier, notwithstanding the fact that at the time of his matriculation he is obliged by the university to sign all kinds of agreements—among them, not to drink beer or fight a duel.

Our hero's share of duels was twenty-eight, generally terminating happily for him, save one of which he still bears the scar upon his left cheek.

Anecdotes abound of the student-life of Bismarck, yet too great credit is hardly to be lent to them; besides, they offer little of general interest except in so far as they afford illustrations of the logical development of the two essentials of his character: namely, humour and an extraordinary sympathy with animals; a sympathy possessed in common with nearly all great humorists, being the natural extreme of their contempt for humankind. Dogs—always large dogs, for he is interested only in those whose features have somewhat of the human, whose fiery eyes attest to a life fiercely ardent as his own—dogs figured in all his adventures. He substituted them for himself or himself for them, indifferently, according to the nature of the escapade. When they appeared upon the scene together the dog snapped, the student supplied the gestures—or the reverse.

The history of his first conflict with the Rector of the University is worthy of being repeated. Bismarck was celebrating, by a banquet, his election to the membership of the " Hannovera " corporation. The drinking was heavy, as always under such circumstances, and Bismarck, in the course of an animated discussion flung an empty bottle out of the window. A passer-by, whom it had doubtless struck, lodged a complaint, and, as the *fête* had been given in the house in which Bismarck lived, our student was summoned to appear before the Rector. He was still in bed when the summons was brought him, with this superscription: " Dominus von Bismarck."

The young *dominus* rose, arrayed himself in his dressing-gown, slipped his feet into his regimental boots, donned his cylindrical (sic) head-covering, and in this singular attire presented himself, pipe in mouth and followed by his great English dog, before the Rector's door. The Rector, terrified at the approach of the huge brute, barricaded himself behind his desk and began by condemning the young *dominus* to the payment of five *thalers'* fine, that he might learn to present himself before the Academic Tribunal in more conventional garb. In the course of the interrogatory, Bismarck, having pretended that the bottle which had fallen into the street might have found its way there unassisted, and offering to demonstrate the truth of the assertion with the ink-bottle, the latter concluded by ordering him to the cell for three days.

Bismarck must have made intimate acquaintance with the cell, for he assures us that he spent there seventeen days, as many at Berlin as at Göttingen. A door is still shown at Göttingen whereon is very legibly inscribed the name of Bismarck; it should be added, however, that as sixty-six years have since elapsed, some biographers venture to doubt the authenticity of this witness.

The "Hannovera"—of which Bismarck had become one of the most distinguished members, both as a drinker and as a fighter—held its meetings either at the inn of the "Vieille Mésange" or at Mardewal's Garden, following the custom which obliges the local seat of all corporations of German students to be invariably a beer-shop. There the costume was sufficiently *bizarre*. It consisted of a short jacket of blue or black velvet or of red plaid, and was completed by a pair of formidable boots, often provided with spurs, and a tiny cap of the colours of the province to which the student belonged.

Bismarck had taken a vizored cap, a black jacket and varnished boots. Is not it related, *à propos* of the last, that the young student had threatened to have his boot-maker devoured by his dog if the boots were not delivered in twenty-four hours? The unhappy boot-maker must have passed the night at work, stimulated, besides, by the sinister voice of Bismarck as he from time to time prowled around the shop, reminding him of the fate which awaited him; and all because the young man had declared to his friends that he should have his boots on the morrow, and did not wish to be given the lie. This anecdote in its entirety is related in the "Dictionnaire Larousse," in which I am astonished to find such lightly-chosen examples; for if the story of the boots is apocryphal (and the rarity[1] of German versions seems to prove it) it is a pitiable invention; if authentic it lacks interest from the fact that so coarse a trait has no psychological value.

Of much more worth, certainly, is the story which Bismarck himself relates, of his wager relative to the unity of Germany.

"It was, I remember," he said to Herr Busch, "toward 1833.

"I had made a wager with a friend in the 'Hannovera,' an American, as to whether or not in twenty years Germany would be united. The winner agreed to pay twenty-five bottles of champagne to the loser, who, himself, was condemned to cross the Atlantic. I naturally wagered the unification. Well, the twenty years having passed in 1853, I recalled this wager, and, as I had lost, I thought of seeking my old University chum in America; but he was dead. As a matter of fact the name he bore did not promise a long life; it was something like Coffin—Sarg."[2]

"The marvel is, however, to think that even in 1833 I should have had something like a presentiment of that unification which to-day is an accomplished fact."

It does seem marvellous indeed; and it is the first time that Bismarck is found to contradict his fundamental theory which, denying the existence of providential men, makes chance the essential factor of political events, thus removing them from all human prevision.

As has been said, during the two half-years passed at Göttingen, Bismarck fought no less than twenty-eight duels. Moreover, he served as witness in an encounter with pistols,

---

[1] Frederic von Koppen reports it, but under a very different form, and assigning to it a date posterior to the university period; moreover, the dog plays no part in his version.

[2] Sarg signifies, in German, coffin.

for which he was summoned before the Academic Tribunal and condemned to ten days' incarceration, in spite of the explanations by which he endeavoured to convince his judges that the favorable issue of the duel was due solely to his intervention.

From that time he was narrowly watched by the Council, which profited by this first affair to forbid his duelling for the future, upon pain of expulsion. He was thus forced to content himself with the part of spectator; even in this quality he was condemned to three days in the cell for having encouraged by his presence a series of illicit acts.

An existence so agitated was good neither for study nor for the student. Bismarck has often since declared that his sojourn in Göttingen appeared to him as a black point in his youth. "The veritable cause of the evil," he one day said, "was my affiliation with the Hannovera Society, which obliged me to lead a life which, left alone, I should perhaps not have followed, and which even obliged me to run into debt. For years the memory of the trifling debts contracted at Göttingen has pursued and saddened me; from which I conclude that, were I obliged to imitate the students of to-day, my entire life would not suffice in which to exhaust my remorse."

Later, in 1885, Bismarck was heard to express the same sentiment to a delegate who had brought him, as an anniversary gift, a collection of his official notes taken at the University. "It is not without chagrin," said he, "that I recall that period of my life; and I am persuaded to-day that the Academic Tribunal showed me an indulgence exceeding my desert."

The last months of his sojourn at Göttingen were signalized by an adventure which must have contributed not a little to his decision, made shortly after, to finish his studies at Berlin.

The students at Jena, having heard of his exploits, and being desirous of making his acquaintance, sent him a formal invitation to visit them. Bismarck, much flattered, arrived in Jena with his friend von Trotha, and both spent there some days and nights of uninterrupted festivity. But one morning while Bismarck was still in bed he received a visit from the beadle of the University of Jena, who respectfully announced to him a decree of the Academical Council, requiring him and his friend to quit the city immediately; the Council claiming that they were corrupting the youth of the University of Jena.

The "Thuringian Society," of which Bismarck was the guest, resolved to protest against this expulsion while preparing for the two young men a triumphant exodus. To this end they hired a landau drawn by six horses. The delegates of the society seated themselves in the carriage, placing the two visitors between them; they were thus conducted beyond the city gates, escorted by their numerous colleagues singing at the top of their voices the *Gaudeamus igitur*.

Never did Bismarck's health suffer from these orgies. The iron constitution with which the young Pomeranian giant was then blessed was proof against every excess, leaving to the chancellor the care of paying the debts of the student. Once only, during his second term at Göttingen, was he overtaken by a slight gastric fever and obliged to summon a physician, by whom quinine was prescribed; but the prescription arriving at the same time with a consignment of sausages and goose pâtés from Kniephof, Otto von Bismarck preferred to administer a dozen sausages, and recovered in spite of them.

At the end of the year 1833 Bismarck asked for his *excat*, and it was with profound relief, as may be readily supposed, that the Rector of the University of Göttingen signed it. It was, moreover, accompanied by remarks hardly flattering to himself. He had still some days of incarceration uncompleted, but by special favour he was permitted to finish the term at Berlin, to which University he removed in order to conclude his studies.

Vacation and a change of air greatly benefited the young man; he reached Berlin in the best spirits yet still with little apparent inclination to follow the course with a more examplary assiduity. The celebrated Savigny at that time occupied one of the most important chairs at the University of Berlin. It was not until the beginning of 1835 that he determined to take a coach and attack his examinations; the subjects had then to be mastered with prodigious haste. Nevertheless he obtained his degree and on the fourth of June, 1835, was appointed *auscultator* at the *Stadtgericht*.

III.

First Humorous Trait of the *Auscultator* Bismarck—A Recalcitrant *Divorcée*—The Worldly Bismarck—A Lesson in Hospitality Given to an Attaché of Embassy—Military Service—Bismarck Saves the Life of His Stable-Boy, and Obtains a Medal for Life-Saving—His Natatory Feats—Bismarck, Gentleman-Farmer—The Legend of the *Tolle Yunker*. The "*Chevaliers de la Désœuvrance*"—Period of Informal Correspondence—Singular Fox-Chase—The Cares of a Farmer—Cynicism or Humour?—How a Good Peace is Concluded—Bismarck Abandons an Administrative Career—A Love Idyl—An Impatient Fiancée—Bismarck is Married to Fraulein Jeanne von Puttkamer—His Capabilities as a Nurse—Children and Grandchildren of the Chancellor.

Up to this time the real soul of Otto von Bismarck had been silent as that of his dogs; subdued by the factitious truculency of the student. It was not until after his return to the place of his birth that it began to awaken, to expand and take its flight toward the proud summits of humorous sentimentality, when the eyes of the young country gentleman would fill with tears of emotional piety at sight of a plough! for at heart he was but an obstinately faithful slave, a watch-dog, endowed with intellectual faculties of the highest order and with a genial egoism.

But the moment for re-entering the fold was not yet. The *auscultator* was to serve his juridical apprenticeship at Berlin, where, this time, he established himself in the family apartment in the Bährengasse, already occupied by his brother Bernard who had just resigned his post of officer of the guard, in order to prepare for his examination as referendary.

Otto at first took his duties very seriously, displaying an even exaggerated zeal in their discharge, if one may believe the following anecdote, not devoid of a certain *vis comica*.

One day, outraged by the intemperate language and disrespectful attitude of a client, Otto von Bismarck sprang from the seat which he occupied and flung at the impertinent fellow this menace—scarcely appropriate to the dignity of the place:

"Choose your words more carefully, sir, or I will kick you out!"

This digression was justly displeasing to the presiding judge who, besides, considered that the young man was rather overstepping the bounds of his prerogative.

"Pardon, Herr *auscultator*," protested the judge, with asperity, "kicking people out is my concern."

The interrupted discussion continued with animation and again the defendant's language became offensive.

"Once more," cautioned Bismarck, angrily, "choose your words more carefully, sir, or I will have you kicked out by the *Stadtgerichtsrath*."

In another circumstance this same readiness of wit, accompanied by the most persuasive, the most conciliatory arguments, was brought to nought by the obstinacy of a married woman who demanded an unconditional separation. Remonstrated with by Bismarck and one of his colleagues in turn, who boasted that he should succeed where the younger man, doubtless for lack of experience, had failed, the woman persisted in her demand and the judges were obliged to yield. Bismarck has pretended that this incident, opening his eyes to the insufficiency of all worldly justice, contributed somewhat to his disillusionment as to his new career.

Between times the young *auscultator* was very mundane; and as he was both a good talker and an elegant dancer the

Bismarck.

salons of Berlin contended for the privilege of receiving him. Among the cosmopolitan aristocracy particularly, he was highly appreciated for the correctness as well as the facility with which he spoke English and French.

Yet the worldly element was not his ideal, for there, too, his taste for jokes of doubtful propriety led him to play pranks which were rather damaging to his reputation as a dandy.

For instance, that ridiculous history of the bread-and-butter sandwiches, by which he essayed the giving of a lesson in hospitality to the master of a house at which he was a frequent visitor. This man, an attaché of a certain embassy, gave frequent balls; brilliant, animated, but innocent of a buffet. The omission was not to the liking of Otto von Bismarck, whose appetite, still celebrated, was aggravated by his exertions as a dancer. He finally agreed with his companions upon a method of apprising the host of his shortcomings in the matter of a buffet. One evening when the ball was in full swing, at a given signal each one of these gentlemen drew from his pocket a bread-and-butter sandwich and began eagerly demolishing it before the eyes of his scandalized partner.

The lesson was heeded, but those who gave it were called upon to apply to themselves the *sic vos non vobis* of the Latin poet; for, as a matter of fact, there was a buffet at the next ball, only those young men were not invited.

At the end of a year Otto von Bismarck was named Referendary to the Royal Tribunal of Aix-la-Chapelle, whence he passed to that of Potsdam, then to that of Griefswald, that he might follow the course in agronomy given by the near-by faculty of Eldena. All that is known of him at this period is that his reserved, disdainful, even haughty character, disconcerted his superiors as it kept at a distance his inferiors and his equals.

The affairs of the landed proprietors, hardly in brilliant shape since the invasion of the French, began to look perceptibly worse. The death of Madame von Bismarck in January, 1839, having reunited the two brothers under the paternal roof, it was decided that they should undertake the administration of the Pomeranian estates and attempt to improve their cultivation. The plan was put into execution the following Easter, the date at which Otto's conditional appointment expired. Herr von Bismarck, Sr., returned with his daughter to Schönhausen, giving up his other estates to his two sons, thereafter united in the struggle against the disaster which threatened to overtake the family property.

This association was painful at the start, the financial situation of the two brothers being most involved. Other biographers have little to say of this troublous time, preferring to exhibit Bismarck as utilizing his leisure in cultivating his knowledge of military tactics; that is, lavishing periods of instruction, as an officer of reserves.

Upon one of these occasions, on the way to Lippehne with a squad of Uhlans, his stable-man, Hildebrand, ordered to bathe the horses, was on the point of drowning in the rather deep waters of the Wendelsee. Seeing the danger, Bismarck, who was watching the performance from one of the bridges, without divesting himself of his uniform or even drawing off his gloves, plunged head foremost into the little lake and rescued the man from certain death.

This exhibition of coolness, courage, noble devotion, was commended in the "Lippehner Chronick" of the time in terms sufficiently emphatic, for it was an example of which the country gentlemen of that period were not prodigal. It also procured for Bismarck a medal for courage, *à propos* of which he afterward made some of his customary facetious remarks.

Perhaps it is not here out of place to recall the fact that

the natatorial talents of Bismarck were developed at Plamann Institute where the Pestalozzi method obtained of *forcing* the children to leap headforemost into the Spree. For the new-comers, the very young ones, who resisted, it took the form of a practical joke, the youngsters and the attendant himself considering it great fun to make them swallow a mouthful of water—even several mouthfuls, as an initiative. When the young Otto arrived at the Institute the pupils, arguing from his timid and reserved air, promised themselves their usual sport, but at the first river-bath which the school took the little Otto mounted the diving board and fearlessly plunged into the water, under the eyes of his discomfited companions.

The moment came, at last, when he was to be enabled to quench his thirst for liberty and independence, for his brother Bernard married and established himself with his wife at Naugard, whence he was to direct the Landsrath.

Otto von Bismarck alone administered the estates of Kniephof and Jarchelin, while his brother reserved for himself Külz, the domain nearest to Naugard.

Then was revealed a Bismarck entirely different from the one which had been known up to this time. The emptiness of his existence weighed upon him; his isolation preyed upon his mind; to escape from it he abandoned himself to physical excesses, becoming the hero of a legend which clung to him even to the time of his marriage. There followed a series of hunting-parties, of infernal raids, of orgies which, if his chroniclers may be believed, were the terror of the countryside for a radius of many miles.

It is permissible to suppose, however, that the dissipations of the future diplomatist did not pass the limit of amusements in which all provincials delight, once they have freed themselves from the restraint of military duty. In "*Ménage de garçon*" Balzac depicts a kind of mysterious association called the "*Chevaliers de la Désœuvrance*" [Knights of Idleness], the members of which, a handful of young scapegraces, employed their strength and intelligence in mystifying and terrorizing the *bourgeois* of Issoudun, their native place. Otto von Bismarck must for some years have led such an existence, only in an infinitely different environment; with all the importance naturally lent to the life of a gentleman-farmer in a country of fertile plains and immense forests.

When, for instance, he trapped foxes to set at large in the peaceable apartment of his cousins, or when he let one of his friends flounder helplessly in a marsh, offering to put a bullet through his head that he might be spared the horrors of imminent drowning, our gentleman-farmer is almost excusable, as consistently playing his rôle of a humorist fatally inclined to violences and exaggerations; he was delightfully incoherent, the most delicate sentiments succeeding coarse jokes, and the one and the other invariably extravagant. He is excused also by the fact that the life which he led upon his always inundated estates, risked becoming mortally wearisome had not it been enlivened by a few such escapades and by the mantle of raillery and humorous causticity which he throws about all things, even the most lugubrious.

We have now reached the epistolary period of Bismarck's life and leave his letters to furnish further enlightenment, particularly as they are full of information as to the successive stages in the career of the future diplomatist. As has been said, these letters are addressed principally to his sister, who had just been married to Herr von Arnim (October, 1844). They are dated, some of them from Kniephof, some from Schönhausen, where from time to time Bismarck spent weeks together with his father. Here is one written on the day after the departure of the young married couple:

After you had gone, the house seemed very lonely. I sat down near the stove to smoke and reflect upon the egoism and unnaturalness of young girls who, having brothers, and what is worse, brothers who are celibates, inconsiderately get married as though they were in the world for the single purpose of following their fabulous caprices; selfishness of which my sex, myself more than all, is happily free.

* * * * * * *

Just now I am stopping here with father. I read, smoke, walk and help him eat his lampreys; then from time to time I play with him a comedy which he calls hunting the fox. We turn out of doors in a pelting rain (and at present with the mercury at six degrees Réaumur) accompanied by Ihle, Bellin and Carl; we tramp through the wood, taking every possible precaution against noise and conscientiously observant of the direction of the wind, although all of us, even, perhaps, father, are convinced that except for an occasional fagot-gatherer there is not a living creature in the wood. Then Ihle, Carl and the two dogs run forward, shouting and barking in a most terrifying manner. Father, with watchful eye and gun charged, stands as still as a statue, as if he really expected to see an animal appear.

Finally Ihle passes him, still shouting excitedly. Turning to me, father naïvely asks if I have not seen something, and I, feigning astonishment, and in a tone which I try to make as natural as possible, reply: " Why no, not so much as could be held in my eye! "

Three or four hours passed in this way, upon each occasion, without the interest of the father, Ihle or Carl wavering for an instant.

Besides this, we visit the orangery twice daily, and the sheepfold once; we inspect every hour the four thermometers in the *salon*, move backward or forward the barometric needles, and since the sun has shone we have succeeded so well in regulating the clocks by it that all strike at the same moment except the one in the library, which is just a trifle slow. Decidedly Charles Fifth was a silly—" *ein dummer Kerl!* "

The Elbe is rising; the wind is from the southwest; the last news from Berlin is that the mercury has fallen to eight degrees Réaumur.

Then after a short interval followed another letter, which enlightens us as to the state of the young man's heart and as to his anxieties as a landed proprietor.

DEAR SISTER: It is with the greatest difficulty that I resist a desire to fill my letter with lamentations over the cultivation of my estate; the nightly frosts, the sick cattle, the unsatisfactory appearance of the colza; the dead lambs, the famished sheep, the scarcity of straw; of fodder, of potatoes, pasture and money. Add to these woes that Jean, out there, is whistling false and without a pause, an infamous schottische; he is evidently endeavouring to cure the pangs of love with his execrable music, which prevents my having the courage to forbid him to whistle. The ideal of his dreams, at the instance of her parents, has just refused his hand and married a wheelwright.

The fact is, I shall have to take a wife myself. I more particularly feel the necessity since father left; I seem to myself utterly alone and abandoned, and the heat and humidity of the atmosphere render me melancholy, and as amorous as lovelorn. It is irresistible; it would appear to be decreed that I shall marry Fraulein———. The world expects it, and as each of us is alone nothing could be more natural. True, she does not love me, but neither am I more impressed with anyone else; it is a good thing not to change one's inclinations with one's shirt—however seldom that feat is accomplished! Father will have told you with what complacence I supported the visits of the women whom I received the first of the month.

Upon my return from Angermünde I found the Hampel overflowed to such an extent that I was unable to reach Kniephof; and as horses were not procurable I was obliged to spend the night at Naugard with several commercial travellers and others who, like myself, were merely waiting for the waters to subside. All the bridges over the Hampel had been carried away so that Knobelsdorf and myself, the

Malvina, Sister of Bismarck.

kings of two great cantons, were confined by the water to a patch of earth while from Schiewelheim to Damm there was none visible. At one o'clock the waters again carried me away in one of my carriages laden besides with three casks of alcohol, and I am proud to be able to say that a carter lost his life in the waves of my tributary, the Hampel.

* * * * * * *

There is no news to tell you, except that my satisfaction in Belein continues; that at this moment, ten o'clock in the evening, the thermometer indicates six degrees above zero; that Odin still limps with his right paw and clings with touching tenderness to the society of Rebecca, which I have chained with him. Good-night, my dear, I send you a kiss. Your brother who loves you, BISMARCK.

It is to be remarked, in passing, that the sprightly humour in these two letters is characteristic of the entire private correspondence of the great man. He is especially apt at seizing the jovial side of things, the comic note in events even the most trifling or pitiful; another peculiarity is that the atmospheric variations so affect and interest this nature-lover, that no matter in what country he may be, the indications of thermometer and barometer are carefully noted in his letters.

Not that he has delicate health; on the contrary, it has always been perfect; and his appetite in proportion to his gigantic stature. He has never dissembled his fondness for good cheer; so little has he sought to do so that all Germany has for years encouraged this taste. During the war of 1870-71, the devotion of his compatriots manifested itself by the supplies of meat and drink which were sent across the Rhine to him; he himself said at table, before Herr Busch, that in order to work well one must be well nourished. "To conclude a fair peace," added the humorist, "I must first have plenty of good things to eat and drink."

In January, 1845, the ex-Referendary was urged to reenter the service of Government. He writes:

It is desired to invest me with the important charge of Superintendent of Dykes; and I am given to hope for a commission for the Saxon Landtag, not, indeed, that of Dresden. Upon the acceptance of the first of these posts will depend the choice of my future abiding-place. This charge is purely honorary, yet it has a certain importance in connection with Schönhausen and adjacent estates, for we sink or swim according as the office is well or ill discharged. On the other hand, my friend C——, who wishes at all costs to send me into Prussia, is trying to procure for me the post of Royal Commissioner for the improvements which are being carried into effect there. Bernard, too, urges me to go; he pretends that I have administrative ability and that it is a career which I shall sooner or later embrace. Cordial greeting to Oscar, Detler, Miss and the other children from your always devoted brother,   BISMARCK.

Nevertheless, Bismarck hesitated; after a few weeks' trial of the position he was about to offer his resignation, when suddenly, early in the autumn, his father died. This time Otto was left entirely alone, and a few months later he accepted the post of Superintendent of Dykes. Let us recollect here that in the partition of property which took place after the death of Otto's father, Otto inherited Kniephof and Schönhausen. Having become châtelain of Varzin in 1867 he resigned Kniephof to Philip von Bismarck, one of his brother Bernard's sons. The estate of Kniephof carries with it the right to a seat in the Chamber of Lords, of which Otto von Bismarck, by an imperial decree, remains the holder during his life.

In the meantime, the love-idyl to which the young country gentleman alluded in an earlier letter, was fashioning itself toward the desired completion; yet not without some discouragements; for the *tolle yunker* had cast his eyes upon a young girl belonging to one of the most haughty families in the country—the Puttkammers. His first meeting with Fraulein Johanna von Puttkammer had occurred two years earlier, at the marriage of his friend and neighbour, Maurice von Blankenbourg and Fraulein von Thaden-Triglaff; Otto was speedily charmed by her air of modest reserve and the candour of soul expressed in her blue eyes.

They saw each other again and the young girl signified her approval of his attentions; there yet remained the consent of the parents to obtain. A first effort was unsuccessful. Herr von Puttkammer was stupefied at the audacity of this "harebrained, foolhardy fellow," this "miscreant" who dared aspire to the honour of becoming his son-in-law. But the candid Johanna expressed her preference for the handsome Superintendent of Dykes, who had just been named a Deputy to the Saxon Landtag, and declared her belief in his ability to make her happy. The parents were forced to yield and Otto von Bismarck was invited to present himself at Rheinfeld, the family residence.

Still hesitating, the parents had assumed an added dignity of manner for the interview; but Otto was not thus to be imposed upon; after the first words of greeting the young man drew the fair Johanna into his arms and so proclaimed his rights at the outset.

The marriage was celebrated on July 28, 1847, and the "*cerveau brulé*" became a model husband; the "foolhardy fellow" the most admirable family man, for he adores children!—and the "miscreant" a steadfast upholder of his religious principles. As for Frau von Bismarck, her tender and admiring affection for the master, her blind devotion to the man whose chosen companion she was for nearly fifty years, were justified to the very hour of her death in 1894. This fact should be emphasized, for Herr von Bismarck is one of the rare great men whose domestic sky was never shadowed by a cloud, who has never compromised with his duties as husband and father, and whose private life, in the matters of honour and loyalty, may defy the most rigorous investigation.

Furthermore, the first years of his marriage but served to develop the vocation for paternity evidently innate in him; as proof of which this letter to his sister, written in 1850, is all-sufficient. Reading it, one is almost disposed to believe that the humorist Bismarck, with his extravagant jests, his mania for making himself the target for his own darts, has in him after all but the making of a gentle, peaceable nurse.

To Frau von Arnim at Norderney.

Schönhausen, July 28, 1850.

I send you a solemn letter of congratulation upon your birthday, which was the twenty-fourth, I think? You are now really of age, or you would be, had not you the happiness to belong to the feminine gender, the members of which, according to jurists themselves, are never freed from the condition of minors, even when they are married to thick-headed imbeciles! I will explain to you why, in spite of its seeming injustice, it is a very wise institution; but not until, in about fifteen days, you will be within earshot. Johanna, who is still reposing in the arms of Lieutenant Morpheus, should have written you what awaits me: the boy trumpeting in a major key, the girl in a minor one; two youngsters singing in the midst of drenched garments and nursing-bottles and I, prepared to concern myself with all as the father of a family very properly should. I opposed the notion of sending Mariette to the baths, in spite of the counsels of all the mothers and aunts who insist that nothing less than sea-air and salt baths will benefit the poor child. As a result I receive numberless reproaches for my barbarity and my stinginess each time the little one takes cold—and this will continue, perhaps, until she is seventy. "You see!" they will say. "Ah, if Mariette could only have gone to the baths!" The little creature does, indeed, suffer much with her eyes, which weep and close by turns; perhaps the trouble is caused by the cutting of her eye-teeth. Johanna is so concerned on the child's account that I have sent for Dr. von Stendhal to-day.

In ending this chapter I will mention the descendants of the ex-Chancellor, who has become a grandfather spoiled and adored by his grandchildren, who have, some of them, reached man's estate. Frau von Bismarck bore three children: the Countess Maria, who has married Count von Rantzau and has herself borne three sons; and Counts Herbert and Wilhelm, who, while yet very young, participated in the Franco-German war.

IV.

Bismarck, Deputy of Prussia and Champion of the Divine Right of Kings—At Frankfort—Pessimism and Bathing by Moonlight—How Bismarck Got the Best of the Proprietor—Plenipotentiary Extraordinary—Florid Descriptive Style of the Letter-Writer—Towing and Diplomacy—Plenipotentiary Truffles—Across Russia in a Post-Chaise—Bismarck and His Bears at St. Petersburg—Cruel Epigram of Prince Bariatinsky—Bismarck Sick—He is Appointed Ambassador to Paris.

At Venice, during his wedding journey, Bismarck had the good fortune to be presented for the second time to Frederic William IV., King of Prussia, whom he had met only casually at Potsdam. He was invited to the King's table, and, by his violence against the liberal party, attracted the master's attention and conciliated his favour.

Delegate to the Federal Diet of Berlin, sent by the Saxon Landtag, he profited by the troubles of 1848 to place himself at the head of the Prussian Reactionaries, proclaiming openly in the Tribune the conservative and authoritative opinions to which he has all his life adhered—for Bismarck is perhaps the only great political man who has never changed the fundamental principles of his doctrine. It is true he has shifted his diplomatic ground. The famous device originated by him at this period: " Mit Gott, für König und Vaterland " [" With God for King and Country "] might be translated thus: " The country submissive to a King who is only second to God." Only later did he recognize the insufficiency of these two allies, the King and God, and consider necessary the addition of that all-powerful auxiliary—the Army.

In 1849 he had himself elected to the second Prussian Chamber, and during his sojourn in Berlin he founded the "*Gazette de la Croix*," which from the start posed as the resolute defender of "the divine right of kings." In May, 1851, he attended the Diet of Frankfort, whither he had himself sent as the associate of General von Rochow, delegate from Prussia. He was at first ill-received by his colleagues, which is doubtless the reason of the sarcasm with which he speaks of all those "charlatans," as he calls them in the letter an extract of which is published in our preface. The sense of his uselessness, of his powerlessness, of the inferior position which he was forced to occupy, the suspicions of those about him, superinduced a veritable attack of spleen, complicated with a black pessimism which he attempted to overcome by taking numberless baths in the Rhine by moonlight, and by sending to Frau von Bismarck lucubrations in the manner of the following:

The day before yesterday I went to Wiesbaden and reviewed, with a mixture of melancholy and wisdom, the scene of my early follies. May it please God to fill with pure and generous wine this vessel in which the champagne of the twenty-first year uselessly fermented, leaving only insipid lees. Where and how are living at this moment———, and Miss ———? how many are dead with whom I flirted and drank and played! Through how many transformations have my judgments of the world passed! how many things now appear small to me which once seemed great! and how many do I honour now which then I despised! I cannot conceive how a man who devotes any time to reflection and who knows nothing nor desires to know anything, of God, can bear the abuse and the *ennui* of life. I do not know how I should have borne it then. If I were forced to live now without faith in God or you or the children, truly I know not why I should not cast off this life as I would a soiled shirt; yet the greater number of my acquaintances are in just that state of unbelief—and live. When I ask myself what motive there is for living so, for fatiguing, irritating one's self, for intriguing and spying, I have no answer. Do not imagine from this that I am unrelievedly gloomy: on the contrary! it is with me as with the changing autumn foliage; strong and energetic, but touched with melancholy, nostalgia, regret of the forest, the sea, the desert; of you and the children; the whole mingled with the setting sun and Beethoven.

To the installation of the Deputy at Frankfort belongs an anecdote which goes to prove that the budding diplomat had not completely divested himself of the old man, that is to say the student *burschikos*. He was lodging at that time in a very handsome house, but not one of the rooms was provided with a bell. Bismarck called the proprietor's attention to the omission and requested that at least one should be placed in his bedroom.

But the landlord protested it was not his affair, his Excellency might have the bell hung at his own expense.

Bismarck was not to be beaten. The following day, at dawn, a detonation startled the entire household; it had originated in the Deputy's bedroom. When the frightened householder arrived Bismarck said to him serenely:

"Do not be alarmed, it is I who fired off a blank cartridge. Having no bell I took that means of summoning my servant. You will do well to accustom yourself to the sound for I shall be forced to use the same method constantly."

The same day the desired bell was placed in the chamber.

A few months sufficed to enable the Deputy from Prussia to triumph over his enemies and his pessimism, thanks to his adaptability and also to his zealous supporters, such as Herr von Manteuffel, the presiding minister, and to the Prince of Prussia himself, the future Emperor William, who was soon to be god-father to Bismarck's second son, Count William, familiarly called Bill.

By the King's favour he was sent the following year (1852)

upon a special mission to the Emperor, Francis Joseph, à propos of the Zoll-Verein. And this truly extraordinary mission took the young diplomat across Hungary, in which country the Emperor was travelling, and to whom Bismarck was to deliver an autograph letter from Frederic William. He overtook Francis Joseph at Pesth and attended the *fêtes* and the hunts with the Court, which he described most picturesquely, even lyrically, to his wife.

Some of his letters during the period are fifteen pages long and elaborate epistolary efforts, consequently it is impossible to quote them in their entirety. Extracts from them will be given of sufficient length to enable the reader to appreciate the descriptive style. Here is the first letter, dated from Szolnok, June 27, 1852.

In the atlas which you have at hand you will find the map of Hungary. Upon that map you will see a river called the Theiss, and by following it to its source, passing Szegedin you will arrive at a locality called Szolnok. Yesterday I went by train from Pesth to Alberti-Josa, where lives a Prince W—— who has been married to a Princess von M——; I went to pay my respects to her that I might give ——news of her health. This place is situated upon the edge of the Hungarian steppes which stretch between the Danube and the Theiss, and I visited it by pure caprice. I have not been permitted to venture without an escort, as the region is infested with mounted brigands called Betyares, who render the country dangerous to cross. After a comfortable breakfast in the shade of an elm I mounted a board wagon with bundles of straw for seats, and drawn by three moorland ponies; the Uhlans charged their carbines, mounted the ponies and we set off at a gallop. Upon the front seat were Hildebrand, a Hungarian domestic and the driver; this last a peasant with long, dark-brown hair and moustache, a broad-brimmed hat and a shirt which reached only to the stomach, leaving between it and the trousers a broad band of bare brown flesh. The trousers were white and full as a woman's petticoat, and came no lower than the knee; the lower part of the leg and the foot were protected by spurred boots. Picture to yourself a green plateau, level as a table, upon which, at intervals of several miles, nothing is to be seen against the horizon except the great naked shafts of the well-sweeps; wells having been dug that water might be drawn for the half-wild ponies and for the cattle—thousands of brown and white cattle, wild as game, and with horns as long as my arm, and herds of stunted ponies, with coats of long hair, watched by half-naked shepherds armed with sticks like lances;—immense numbers of pigs, each lot accompanied by an ass, the mission of which is to carry the shepherd's coat and, incidentally, the shepherd himself; then vast flocks of bustards and innumerable hares and hamsters; and again, here and there beside a lake of impure water, wild geese, ducks and plovers.

* * * * * * *

I arrived here about five o'clock; that is, at the hour when a motley crowd of Hungarians and others were circulating in the streets of Szolnok. From my lodging I could hear the wildest and most senseless Bohemian melodies. These people sing in a nasal tone, with mouth wide open, and in a minor key, plaintive songs, descriptive of the torments caused by certain black eyes, or of the death of some illustrious brigand. One would swear one heard the wind roaring down the chimney. The women are generally good-looking, some of them even remarkably beautiful. All have jet-black hair arranged with scarlet ribbons. Married women wear on their heads green and red fichus, or coifs of gold-embroidered red velvet, and across the shoulders and breast silk shawls of a beautiful shade of yellow. Besides, they wear short sky-blue skirts and boots of red morocco which reach to the hem; these accessories, with their swarthy brown skins and black eyes, form a picturesque assemblage of striking colours which you would, I am sure, find admirable. A few minutes after my arrival, while awaiting dinner, I took a plunge in the Theiss and watched some native dances. What a pity that I do not know how to draw! I should for your benefit execute some fabulous sketches. I have eaten some fish—and other things, and

Bismarck, when Delegate to the Federal Diet.

drunk a good deal of Hungarian wine, and now I want to go to bed, provided the Bohemian music will let me sleep a little. Good-night. *Istem adiamek!*

BISMARCK.

As a contrast to this picture, almost Oriental, here is a Northern landscape, sketched by a master-hand, while Herr von Bismarck was on a mission to Sweden in 1857.

This quotation anticipates the chronological order adopted by us, but the example will serve to further demonstrate the variety and suppleness of Bismarck's epistolary style. These letters reveal the humorist, the being all intuitions and impressions, to whom the heart of things appeals rather than their externality; their more intimate character more often than their general aspect; and who assimilates more readily the people with whom, and the things with which, he comes in actual contact. As a matter of fact his descriptions take the form, nearly always, of a suggested imagery, which energizes inanimate objects. From Amsterdam he wrote in 1853: "The chimneys look like men standing on their heads, with legs and arms spread far apart." Another time, alluding to a Swiss landscape, our epicure compared it to "a dish of cabbage garnished with eggs."

Tromsjoenaes, August 16.

Not a town, not a village as far as the eye can reach; only a few isolated frame huts with a little barley and a few potatoes about them, lost among stunted trees, rocks and weeds. Recall the most deserted bit of land in the vicinity of Viartlum [estate in Pomerania belonging to the Puttkammers]; nearly a hundred square miles of tall heather, alternating with vines running along the ground and with marsh-land, with birch, juniper, fir, beech, oak and alder, sometimes thick-clustered, elsewhere scattered sparsely; the whole thickly sown with bowlders, some of them as large as a house and exhaling a fragrance of resin and rosemary; with curiously shaped lakes here and there, fringed with forests and hills of heather; thus you will have an idea of Smaland, where I am at this moment. It is in very truth the country of my dreams; inaccessible to despatches, to my colleagues and to N. N—— (and, unhappily, to you). I should like to possess, beside one of these tranquil lakes, a hunting lodge where I might gather for a few months all my dear ones at present united at Rheinfeld. The winters here are insupportable because of the mud. * * * We have been dining at the hunting-lodge, a curious frame structure situated upon a peninsula extending into the lake. My chamber and the three chairs, two tables and bed are all of the colour of the rough pine of which all the walls in the house are composed. The bed is very hard, yet after so much fatigue one can sleep without being rocked. I see from my window a hill clothed with flowering heather from among which spring saplings which sway in the wind; between them I catch glimpses of the lake, and beyond the lake extends a forest of firs. Beside the house is a tent for the coachmen and other domestics, and the peasants; then come the coach-house and a small canine city composed of eighteen or twenty dog-houses which form a street or alley; and from each kennel hangs the head of a dog tired out with yesterday's hunting.

Returned to Frankfort, the humorist was bored to death with listening to reports of the Diet, "immeasurably fastidious"; yet he wrote his sister that the greater part of his leisure was spent in the chase. Politics leaving him with much time on his hands during most of the year 1853, he imagined himself in need of rest and took his repose in the shape of travel, becoming an enthusiastic tourist. Having obtained leave of absence he consumed the summer and autumn in visiting Belgium, Holland, Westphalia, Italy and Switzerland.

During the years which followed his influence and political authority steadily increased; he was selected for many foreign negotiations and it is entertaining to follow, through his unofficial correspondence, the infinitely varied and grotesque pictures by which he described the progressive steps in his new career of commercial traveller in diplomacy. In principle he deplored his nomadic existence, which he called " vagabondage " ; but as a matter of fact it enchanted him. When he wrote to his wife that he should have preferred to remain in the Chamber of Lords, where, unimpeded by any official hinderance he could " direct politics in his bathing clothes "—" an occupation," he added, " which has always had as great a charm for me as a continuous diet of truffles, dispatches and Grand Crosses, such as diplomacy offers," one may be sure that he meant not a word of it; for in reality his dreams were all of embassies and special missions, and the two poles of the magnet were for the moment Saint Petersburg and Paris; the capitals of the two great nations with which he foresaw the possibility of a definitive alliance fifty years thence, in spite of the Crimean war, terminated by the taking of Sevastopol; in spite of the catastrophes into which his hatred of all that was Gallic soon precipitated France and her saddened Emperor. Saint Petersburg whence, in 1858, he writes to his wife: " I should not be sorry to take refuge in a big bearskin great-coat, with caviare and an occasional stag-hunt, against the inclement political weather which will soon overtake Frankfort." He visited Paris during the Exposition of 1855; a semi-official visit by which he profited to begin throwing dust in the eyes of Napoleon III.

In March, 1859, the first of his dreams was realized. The Prince Royal of Prussia, who had acted as Regent for a year, sent him as Ambassador to the Court of Russia. He posted to Saint Petersburg, a method of conveyance which would hardly justify its being called a pleasure trip, and of which the humorist relates the Odyssey in his usual happy vein.

Russia seemed to lengthen under our wheels, the *versts* to bear little ones at each station; but here we are at last at our railway port. From Königsberg to Pskow we travelled for ninety-six hours without stopping; sleeping only four hours at Kowno and three at the station of Degucie, near Dunabourg. I think that was the day before yesterday. I am now perfectly comfortable except that my skin burns from exposure to the air all night, when the cold varied from one to twelve degrees. The snow was so heavy that we stuck in it in spite of the efforts of our six or eight horses, and we were frequently forced to continue the journey on foot. The slippery bridges in the mountains were still more disagreeable, particularly coming down; it took us an hour to make twenty steps, for the horses fell four times and eight times became entangled in the harness. With all this it was night and the wind was high—a veritable winter journey through nature. It was not possible to sleep sitting up, if only because of the cold; but one is better off in the open air and I shall make up the sleep lost.

Yet the foregoing was but the beginning. As he went on toward Saint Petersburg the snow fell and the trip exhausted itself in indescribable vicissitudes.

At Wirraballan I found a post-chaise which on the interior was too low for my height; I therefore changed places with Angel and completed the distance on the outside seat, which was open in front, a narrow bench of which the back bristled with pointed angles, making it, apart from the cold, impossible to sleep. I supported these conditions from Friday morning until Monday evening, and without counting the first and last nights in the train I did not sleep from Wednesday morning until Tuesday evening, except once for three hours and another time two hours upon a sofa at one of the relay-stations. The skin was peeling from my face when I arrived. The journey occupied a longer time because of the fresh-fallen snow, through which there was no track cut for the sleighs. We were obliged frequently to trudge along on foot when our eight horses could not pull us. The Duna was frozen, but a half-mile above there was a place free from ice, where we crossed. The Wilna was swollen with ice-cakes; the Niemen had none.

Occasionally the supply of horses was exhausted because at each post we were obliged to take eight or ten instead of only three or four, as usual; I never had less than six, yet the carriage was not very heavy. The zeal of the guard, the driver and the postilion was so excessive that I was forced to curb it in order to save their poor beasts unnecessary torture. The icy bridges in the mountains were the principal drawbacks to our progress, particularly in descending them; the four hindmost horses occasionally fell one upon another, a confused, struggling mass; but the postilion, who was mounted upon one of the horses forward on the right, never fell, and the moment the others were on their feet again he started them on a run, the carriage, loaded atop with a quantity of luggage, swaying after as rapidly as the wheels could turn; the whole accompanied by shouts and much cracking of whips. This manner of driving is undoubtedly the wiser for the horses fall only when going slowly.

* * * * * * *

April 1st. As I write this date I am reminded that it is the anniversary of my birth. It is the first time that I have ever heard the ice crack upon this day; and it is the first time in twelve years that I have spent it away from Johanna."

Thus the new Prussian Ambassador was established at Saint Petersburg with his wife, children, horses, dogs and a whole menagerie besides, reinforced by some superb bears which he afterward carried back to Germany. Despite the insufficiency of his salary (thirty thousand *thalers*—twenty thousand dollars) his house was most hospitably maintained, the Ambassadress winning all hearts by her gracious informality of manner; for one did not dine there unless he was satisfied to accept " pot-luck."

Such, at least, is the German version. Other writers have asserted that the diplomatist was successful at Court, but that his personality did not favorably impress the higher circles of Saint Petersburg society. His unyielding character, his brusque, sometimes violent humour, was disapproved and resented. Witness the following anecdote, given in an English journal:

While he was ambassador at Saint Petersburg he, one evening in the *salon* of the Princess Bariatinsky, permitted

Bismarck's Children, Herbert, Wilhelm, and Marie (1854).

himself to give expression to his customary facetious reflections upon various political personages who chanced to be absent, turning against them the most biting epigrams; his hostile attitude perceptibly chilled the social atmosphere.

As his Excellency left the house a dog in the court-yard

began to bark furiously. Prince Bariatinsky could not resist the pleasure of retaliating upon the guest who had been so ill-humoured all the evening, by opening the window and exclaiming, apprehensively:

"*Monsieur l'ambassadeur*, do not bite my dog, I beg of you!"

A journey which the new ambassador made to Moscow early in June was not less interesting than that to Saint Petersburg, and is described with unimaginable picturesqueness.

Green is quite deservedly the favorite colour of the Russians. Of the hundred miles which I traversed to reach this place I passed about forty asleep; but the sixty remaining presented in every direction a succession of shades of green. Except the railway stations I saw neither houses nor villages, nor yet towns. Forests of birch, forming an impenetrable thicket, cover the marshes and hills. A magnificent plant springs at the foot of the trees, which are occasionally separated by long stretches of prairie; and this appearance continues through ten, twenty, forty miles. I do not recall having seen any fields or heather or sand. Cows or horses passing, solitary, now and then, led one to suppose that there might be men in the neighborhood. Moscow seen from above looks somewhat like a recently sown field. The soldiers are green, the cupolas are green, and I doubt not the hens are green that have laid the eggs upon my table. You would probably like to know why I am here; I have asked myself the same question, replying that change is the soul of living. The truth of this profound maxim is the more readily recognized when one has been spending ten weeks in a hôtel chamber exposed to the sun and looking out upon the paved street. The delights of changing one's domicile pall when such changes occur frequently in a short time; I, therefore, determined to renounce them. I confided all my papers to ——; I gave my keys to Angel; I announced that in eight days I should be at the Stenbock's, and I set out for the station to go to Moscow. This people has the habit of harnessing slowly and driving rapidly. I ordered the carriage two hours ago and each time that I have asked for it at intervals of ten minutes for the last hour and a half the answer has been: "Directly!" with amiable imperturbability; you know with what exemplary patience I can wait—but there is a limit to everything. And, once started, the horses travel such a pace that they break down, the carriage goes to pieces upon the rough roads and the journey has to be concluded on foot. While waiting I have drank three cups of tea and eaten several eggs. The efforts of the domestic to make the fire burn are succeeding so well that I am beginning to feel the necessity for some fresh air. I should shave myself if I had a mirror.

Upon his return to Saint Petersburg he surveyed his position with satisfaction. His work was nice rather than difficult. There were forty thousand Prussians to whom he was expected to serve as detective, advocate, judge, captain of recruits and sub-prefect. Every day brought some fifty signatures to make, passports to despatch and visits to pay; all which in no wise hindered the course of diplomacy. Bismarck followed with unquiet eye the digressions of Prussian politics which, he said, was sinking more and more deeply into the Austrian furrow. Even then he predicted the Franco-Prussian war, in which Austria would or would not lend her aid, according to the dictates of self-interest.

As God wills, he concludes. Here it is but a question of time; peoples and individuals, folly and wisdom, war and peace, all are unstable as the waves: the sea rests. There is nothing on earth but hypocrisy and jugglery. Whether fever or rifle ball tear the mask from one's face it must fall soon or later. Then will there be discovered between a Prussian and an Austrian, if they are of equal height, a resemblance which will make it difficult to distinguish one from the other. For the matter of that, imbeciles and wise men, reduced to skeletons, are alike as two drops of water. It is certain that specific patriotism will not stand the test; but one must despair were we reduced to that precarious dependence.

This extract is bitterly pessimistic, for the humorist has permitted a glimpse of the depths of his nature, which is sad even in spite of his jests and sarcasms. Yet let the man whom we have seen happy up to this moment, be touched by sorrow, and his pen becomes veritably pathetic; he writes the most beautiful letters which the tender compassion of a heart like his can inspire. Such is the letter which he addressed to his brother-in-law, the husband of his sister Malvina, upon learning of the death of one of their children (August, 1861).

I have just heard of the frightful misfortune which has overtaken you and Malvina. My first thought was to go to you at once, but I overestimated my strength. The cure has weakened me, and my decision to interrupt it suddenly has encountered such energetic opposition that I have concluded to let Johanna go to you alone. No human consolation can touch such a grief, yet there is a natural desire to be near those one loves, when they are suffering, and to mingle one's tears with theirs. That is all we can do. You could hardly have a greater sorrow; so to lose so lovable a child who was progressing promisingly, and to bury with him all the hopes which, realized, should have been the joy of your declining years, is a chagrin which will be yours so long as you are on earth; I feel it by the profound and sorrowful compassion with which your trouble inspires me. We are in God's hands and can but bow to his will. He may take back all that he has given us, leave us entirely alone, and the affliction will seem but the more cruel if we permit our woe to degenerate into reproaches and revolt against his omnipotence. Do not allow upon your legitimate grief the intrusion of one bitter thought, one rebellious murmur; remember that there still remains to you a son and a daughter and that with them you may be happy even while tenderly recalling the beloved child whom you kept with you for fifteen years; compare your lot with those who have never had children, never known the joys of paternity. I would not importune you with my feeble consolation, but assure you only that as your friend and brother I feel your grief as profoundly as though it were my own. How trivial seem the little cares and disagreements of our daily life beside a real misfortune; and how frequently I reproach myself for the complaints and desires to which I have so often given expression because I was forgetful of all the happiness God gives us and all the dangers which surround without touching us! We should not become enamoured of this life and imagine ourselves at home; in twenty years or thirty, at most, we shall be quit of the cares of this world, and our children, having reached our present age, will realize with amazement that their life, still so novel and delightful, is already declining. Were this life indeed the end it would not be worth the trouble of dressing and undressing. Do you recollect those words of a travelling companion of Stolpemünde? By thinking of death as the passage into another life you will more easily master your grief, for you will say to yourself that your dear child will be your faithful companion as long as you live. Our circle of loved ones diminishes, rather than enlarges, when there are no children. At our age one does not contract ties capable of replacing those that are broken. Let us then be still more closely united until death shall separate us one from the other as it has separated us from your son. Who knows that it may not be soon?

That point of interrogation proves for the second time that the only event which Bismarck's spirit of divination failed to foresee was his own longevity.

Nevertheless the climate was unfavourable to the health of the Prussian Ambassador. He fell seriously sick and did not entirely recover. With the mania for self-mockery which had become characteristic, Bismarck relates, *à propos* of this sickness, that someone gravely called his attention to the fact that all the representatives from Prussia to Russia had either died or gone mad. Yet, while deploring his nomadic existence and asserting that change of residence is half death, he began to sigh for a post at London, Paris or Berlin. He even wrote his sister that he would drink a bottle of fine wine on the day when he should have in his pocket his appointment to Paris. And as everything succeeds with him, he obtained it in May, 1862.

V.

Bismarck at Paris in 1862—Hôtel of the Legation—Criticism of the Appearance of the Emperor and Empress—Fresh Access of Spleen, Bismarck Feels Lonely in Paris—Promenades in the Bois and at Saint-Germain—A *Mot* of Guizot-Album Sentiment—Bismarck Recalled to Berlin and Made President of the Council—Epicureanism, Hunting, and Overwork—A Price Set Upon Prince Bismarck's Head—The Attempt of the Student Blind—Bismarck is Photographed With a Singer—His Remorse—Sadowa—The Stroke of the Spur—Triumph of the Bismarckian Policy—Napoleon III. Declares War Against Prussia.

During a brief stay in Paris in 1857, Bismarck, stopping at the Hôtel de Douvres, wrote his sister:

I have five chimneys, yet I am freezing; five clocks, all ticking, yet I never know the hour; eleven large mirrors, yet my cravat is always ill-tied.

The Prussian ambassador seemed little better satisfied with his installation in 1862. The hôtel of the Legation is well-located, but gloomy, damp and cold, as he says in a letter addressed to his wife.

The south side is occupied by the staircase and the *non-valeurs;* all is exposed on the north and is haunted by an odour of mustiness and sewage. There is no furniture, no corner where it is a pleasure to sit down; three-quarters of the house, consisting of *salons*, is closed, and the furniture swathed in covers which are not expected to be disturbed. The maids occupy the third floor, the children the second; the first consists only of a bed-room in which is a great bed, a few out-of-date parlours (style of 1818) and numerous staircases and antechambers. One lives in the *rez-de-chaussée*, north side, near the garden, where I sun myself at most three times a week, for several hours. Besides, on the main floor, there is but one bed-chamber. All the domestic affairs are transacted on the second floor, which is reached by a dark, narrow, steep staircase, up which my broad shoulders will not admit of my walking straight (even although I wear no crinoline). The principal staircase extends only to the first floor. Two others, one at either end of the house, straight and narrow as ladders, lead to the upper stories. Here Hatzfeld and Pourtales lived all the time, but they died in the very flower of their age; and if I remain in this house I shall die too. I should not lodge here even if I might do so for nothing, if only because of the ill odour.

When the new Ambassador presented his credentials he was, as always, most amiably received by the Emperor, although it was an official ceremony to which his Excellency was brought in the usual state, in a Court carriage.

Bismarck found the Emperor looking well; he had become stronger, but was neither fatter nor coarser, as all the caricatures paint him. The Empress, Bismarck still thought one of the most beautiful women he knew, even after Saint Petersburg.

Meanwhile his Excellency was bored to death, and for the first time in many years was not sufficiently occupied; in the rare letters which he wrote he was rather morose; complained of the rain, of being obliged to dine alone, of not knowing whom to visit.

Although I am in the midst of great Paris, I feel more alone than do you at Rhinefeld, and I am hidden like a rat in this deserted house. The only pleasure I have had has been the discharge of the cook because of the extravagance of her accounts—and you know my indulgence in that particular. I sometimes eat at the *café;* God knows how long that will last. In eight or ten days I shall probably be sum-

Jeanne de Puttkamer, Wife of the Chancellor.

moned by despatch to Berlin and things will become serious.

In short, Bismarck's moral barometer, which was always influenced by atmospheric variations, was "set stormy." He wrote July 14th, after a trip to London which made him better appreciate Paris:

We have had fine weather since yesterday; until then the cold was intense and the rain incessant. I profited by the change to dine at Saint Germain; it is in the midst of a beautiful forest, with a terrace overlooking the Seine, from which is had a magnificent view of woodland, mountains, towns and villages. Every place is buried in verdure; I have just been driving in the Bois by the softest moonlight; thousands of carriages were there; the lakes were covered with coloured lights and there was an open-air concert. Now I am going to bed.

Bismarck remained in Paris just long enough to permit Napoleon III. to pronounce the most profound words to which he ever gave utterance: of Bismarck he said: "He is not a serious man." Would it had pleased God that the man of the Second of December had treated the Prussian Diplomatist with more consequence instead of as he did—a policy which Bismarck designated as "*politique de pourboire.*"

M. Guizot, however, was not at all of the Emperor's opinion; we find in an article in the "Révue des Deux Mondes" (1866) these words, equally profound:

"At this hour there is but one ambitious and daring man in Europe, and that man is Bismarck."

Which proves once more that when reference is made to a man so many-sided in character, the most divergent opinions, the most contradictory judgments may be reconciled. And since we are upon sentences and aphorisms let us mention an album of thoughts signed by the Prussian Ambassador while in Paris. His colleague, Count Inzenberg, *chargé d'affaires* of Hesse, and a great collector of autographs, possessed an album wherein the political personages of the day were invited to inscribe a few original lines. Anecdotal history has detached from this album a page upon which is to be found the three "thoughts" which follow, written one under the other.

"During my long career I have learned to pardon much and often, but I have forgotten nothing. Guizot."

"A little lack of memory cannot detract from the sincerity of the pardon. Thiers."

"As for me, existence has taught me to forget many things and to pardon many more. von Bismarck."

Four months after his arrival in Paris Bismarck was recalled to Berlin, where the evil times which he had predicted had arrived. The Prince of Prussia, having become King, was at odds with his Assembly upon the subject of military reorganization. The Cabinet had resigned and it was then that the King called to his assistance the man who was more royalist than himself; the implacable foe to all parliamentary liberty; the iron arm which was to overcome the Chamber, the country, Germany entire by the might "which precedes right," and who, even before his departure for Russia, spoke of curing the infirmities of the Confederation by iron and fire ("ferro et igne").

Herr von Bismarck was made President of the Cabinet, and from that time his political star began to shine with extraordinary lustre, little reassuring, however, for the peace of Federal Germany.

The new President-Minister established himself very comfortably at Berlin, happy to know himself at last in his proper element; proud also to plant himself at the feet of his royal master. Foreseeing that he should be overdriven, like a true apostle of the "mens sana in corpore sano," he thought only of living well, and gave a loose rein to his epicurean tastes. On October 10th, or about three weeks after his arrival in Berlin, he wrote to his sister:

I have never eaten such excellent pudding and rarely liver so good. Blessed be culinary masterpieces! I have breakfasted upon them now three days. Cook Rimpe has come and I eat alone at home, when I do not dine at his Majesty's table. My sojourn in Paris agreed with me. At Letzlingen I shot a stag, a wild sow, four stags "à tête paumée," five brockets, four fallow-deer; nevertheless I missed many good shots; while my neighbors missed more than I. Here, work is daily increasing. To-day from eight till eleven, diplomacy; from eleven until half-after two, conferences with several ministers; report to the King until four; from half-after four until a quarter before five a gallop in the rain to the Hippodrome; dinner at five; from seven until ten, that is, till now, work of all kinds. But withal good health, good sleep and strong thirst.

It would be unjust not to add that he who, from then on, was to direct the policy of Prussia and precipitate it into war, did so at his own peril. The Prussianizer [!] of Germany was to become terribly unpopular.

In 1866, at the campaign of Sadowa, he was so bitterly execrated that a German journal published an announcement in which a certain Dr. J. Hundegger offered "a prize of 100 florins to the soldier who will obtain possession of the person of Count von Bismarck, dead or alive." (Bismarck was elevated to the rank of Count after the Convention of Gastein in August, 1865.)

In that same year (May 5, 1866) occurred the attempt of the student Blind. Bismarck, having left the Royal Palace, was crossing the Avenue des Tilleuls when two pistol shots echoed behind him; as he turned three more shots followed, the last grazing his shoulder; he seized his assailant by the wrist and succeeded in holding him until the officers appeared.

Blind declared that he intended only to save Germany by suppressing "the instigator of a fratricidal war." Some days after he committed suicide in prison, and German public opinion was so violently excited against Bismarck that the wives of high officials placed flowers upon the student's grave.

This chapter shall terminate with an amusing anecdote, relative to the various sojourns which Bismarck made at Gastein during the negotiations of the convention which was to regulate the Duchies of Schleswig-Holstein and Lauenburg; an anecdote authenticated by the accompanying photograph.

One day while the President-Minister was walking in the park at Gastein he met the celebrated singer, Pauline Lucca (Countess von Rahden).

"You look very gloomy," said Pauline Lucca.

"One cannot always be gay," replied Bismarck; "and as for me, I have no reason to feel so just now."

"Well," suggested the actress, "come and be photographed with me; that will distract you for at least a few moments."

Bismarck acquiesced, and this was the origin of the photograph which is still in existence at Friedrichsruh, and below which the Chancellor has written: "Art is pleasant, life is serious."

This photograph made a great scandal in Germany.

To his friend, André de Roman, who reproached him for the foolishness, he replied by a long homily pointed with irony, from which I extract the following curious passage:

Madame von Rahden, although a singer, is a woman whom no one can accuse (with more truth than I could be accused) of ever maintaining illicit relations; nevertheless, had I, even at the last moment, weighed the possibilities of chagrin which this pleasantry might cause many sincere friends, I would have retired beyond the range of the ob-

Bismarck and Pauline Lucca (Ischl, 1865).

jective directed upon us. * * * But your friendship and your own belief in Jesus Christ, make me hope that you will recommend me to the clemency of my judges, for all of us have need of it. I hope that among the many sinners who do not vaunt their piety, God will accord me also his grace and not deprive me, in the midst of the doubts and dangers of my mission, of the support of the humble faith with which I seek my path.

* * * * * * *

The war which Bismarck had been years in preparing was finally declared, and the victory of Sadowa consecrated the

Bismarck in his Study.

triumph of his policy. Attired in his uniform of cuirassier of the *landwehr*, Bismarck fought through the entire campaign by the King's side. His biographers report concerning this fact a typical incident. At Sadowa, the shells bursting very near the monarch, Bismarck invited him to seek a place of safety, but the King objected that, being Generalissimo of the army, his place was in the midst of his men. The situation having become untenable, Bismarck insisted, observing that, as President of the Cabinet he was responsible for the life of his Sovereign and consequently had the right to exact that it should not be uselessly exposed. The King yielded to this reasoning and turned his horse's head; but as the animal walked too slowly to suit Bismarck, he, disengaging his foot from the stirrup, surreptitiously gave the horse a violent dig with his spur, which had the result of promptly carrying the King and his minister out of harm's reach. One hour later the Prussian bugles proclaimed victory.

The political events which signalized the years which followed and terminated in the regrettable event of the Franco-German war, are not our affair. Hence they will be merely mentioned in this place.

Bismarck had replied to Napoleon III.'s appreciation of him, "That man is not serious," by saying that the Emperor was but a romantic fool. This, too, was a true estimate, for from 1866 Napoleon III. aged, grew stupid, lost vivacity, committed fault upon fault and fell like a child into every trap the Prussian diplomatist set for him.

Perceiving rather late that it had been a mistake to crush Austria, he engaged in a "*politique de pourboire*," asked compensation, offered to Prussia an alliance, offensive and defensive, in exchange for the cession of the Luxembourg, the Palatinate and Hesse (Mayence included). But Bismarck had no interest in concluding that alliance; he felt that war with France was inevitable if the unification of Germany was to be achieved by grouping under one flag, in times of danger, the northern and southern states. He continued to oppose to the exactions of the Emperor that dilatory policy which he had hitherto found so successful, while he quietly assured himself of the neutrality of Austria and Italy and accomplished the isolation of France in the event of war.

Napoleon III. compromised himself more and more deeply; encouraged by the half-victory of the evacuation of the Luxembourg, he held back in the affair of Schleswig, even recommending Prussia to annex Saxony by force; and finally, when there remained but one more blunder to commit, that of assuming the responsibility of a declaration of war, Bismarck suggested it to him by reviving the candidature of a Hohenzollern to the throne of Spain.

The conciliatory disposition of the King of Prussia in this affair is well known. Upon steps taken by the French Ambassador and at the instance of M. de Grammont, acting on behalf of the Emperor, the candidature of the Hohenzollerns was withdrawn.

Napoleon III., subjugated by his advisers who would have war at any cost, believed it necessary to exact a guaranty for the future, and M. Benedetti was charged to demand it verbally of the King, who was then at Ems. But the King eluded the solicited interview by returning the reply that he had nothing further to communicate upon the subject.

Bismarck amplified the despatch from Ems which announced the King's decision, transmitting it to the foreign cabinet in a form presenting the matter, insignificant in itself, as a humiliating check to France.

Napoleon III. considered that there was then no choice but to declare war against Prussia.

VI.

Hereditary Enemy—"With the Help of God"—Bismarck Campaigning—The Secret of His Insomnia—The Chancellor's Colleagues—Antagonism between the Chancellor and the Army Staff—Bismarck's Criticism of German Generals—Bismarck, Strategist—The Capitulation of Sedan Related by the Chancellor—The Humorous Diplomatist is Checkmated by a Bavarian Gunner.

Bismarck was at last to be enabled to satiate his hatred of France and the French. Hatred born of all the dissemblance of soul which has created between the Gauls and the Teutons an historical and ethnical abyss seemingly impassable; of all which distinguishes the heavy, stiff-backed Prussian soldier from the light, supple trooper of France; hatred which is nourished at the profound sources of intellectual and physical antagonisms, by that which the Germans lack of our *finesse*, our wit, even our courtesy, which Bismarck considers "hypocrisy and envy."

If Bismarck may not be said to be the direct instigator of that war, at least the sly diplomatist sought and provoked it, and assumed all the responsibility thereof, because in his hands have been held, since 1866, the principal pieces in the political game of chess in Europe.

With a light heart he quitted Varzin, a new estate which he had acquired in 1867, after a visit to the Exposition Universelle; a visit by which he had profited to execute his last diplomatical curvets before the Emperor at the Tuileries.

The die was cast! the feudal dog would follow his master and would not return to Berlin until after having strengthened the Imperial crown upon the head of William I.

The unheard-of, the disconcerting fact in all this is the good faith with which he imagined himself playing a providential *rôle*, acting by virtue of a special decree from the God of the Protestants.

'Twas "by God's aid" that he would carry across desolated France his eternal uniform of the cuirassiers (white cap, boots, blue coat and yellow collar); "by God's aid" that he would put Strasbourg to fire and sword; "by God's aid" that he would rain upon the vanquished his jests, his malice, all the arsenal of his Berliner's *witz;* "by God's aid" that he would show himself implacable toward Jules Favre, whose grief was to appear to him artistically painted; finally, it was "by God's aid" that he would crown his work by founding the German Empire upon the ruins of the German Confederation. And one asks one's self, by what strange aberration of mind a man of such lofty intelligence could see the finger of Providence in a succession of phenomena so contrary to Christian morality (his own morality), even to the most elementary principles of social evolution, which proves that every epoch marked by the supremacy of the military type coincides with a general halt in the progress of civilization. Yet perhaps after all, one should see in this affectation of religious fatalism only an unconscious transposition of the spirit of superstition common to all men of genius, or still possibly a reflex manifestation of the Bismarckian humour; of that irrepressible boyishness of temperament which seems to be the common appanage of great dogs and great men.

From beginning to end of this terrible campaign the future Chancellor shared his master's fatigues, manifesting neither wavering nor lassitude. The first encampments were lacking in every comfort; often it was necessary to improvise from various unsuitable articles, the table at which Bismarck breakfasted and dined and transacted the business of the Empire by the flickering light of candles stuck into the necks of empty champagne-bottles. He had frequently to content himself with a mattress upon the ground instead of a bed; and as he could sleep little he worked far into the night, obliging his secretaries and others of his staff to sit with him.

The secret of his insomnia was less the anxieties of war than his habit of inordinate eating and drinking; vices which, six years later, were to bring him to death's door. He admits himself that he has the misfortune to eat and drink incontinently as in his Göttingen days.

"There is always a dish too many," he said at Versailles. "I am resolved to ruin my stomach with *canard aux olives*, and there is still *jambon de Rheinfeld*, which I must eat if only to get my share, because I do not take *déjeuner à la fourchette;* and to crown all we have *sanglier de Varzin!*"

But we will not anticipate. The Chancellor entered upon the campaign with a staff of secretaries and councillors; a somewhat homogeneous collection, for it included gentlemen such as the Baron von Holstein, old revolutionists like Lothar Buscher, and defrocked clerics like Moritz Busch; elements very dissimilar, but which the cleverness of the Chancellor knew how to "lump" as M. Clémenceau would say. The lump in question lodged in the same house with the Chancellor, when circumstances permitted, and ate at the same table.

When Bismarck visited a field of battle or a view he carried a black leather case containing field-glasses and was armed with a sword and a revolver. In the way of decorations he ordinarily wore only the Cross of the Commander of the Red Eagle, to which later was added the Iron Cross.

During the entire campaign Bismarck gave proof of endurance and self-denial, if not of sobriety.

"In travelling," writes Mr. Busch, "our carriages immediately followed those of the King. We started generally about ten in the morning and sometimes accomplished long stages.

"Upon our arrival at the place where the night was to be spent a bureau was established without loss of time, where someone was always at work."

The Church at Schönhausen.

There were notes to take, circulars to draw up, orders to write or copy, telegrams to cipher or decipher; and all was done silently, calmly, with prodigious rapidity; doubly contrasting with the disorder in the German military headquarters and above all, alas! in the French.

Serious antagonism began to display itself between the

The Bedroom of the Chancellor.

Chancellor's staff and that of the King; that is to say, between the civil element and the military. The disguises of these gentlemen—that of Bismarck in the yellow uniform of the cuirassiers, of Kendell in the blue uniform of the cuirassiers, and of Bismarck Bohlen in the uniform of the King's dragoons—were held in slight esteem by the real military men. Rather frequent conflicts, resulting in sullen rivalry, occurred between the diplomatic and the military directors; the latter going so far as even to refuse to communicate certain despatches to the Chancellor. Upon their arrival at the markets the officers chose the best places for themselves. When Verdun capitulated, they neglected even to submit to the Chancellor the treaty of capitulation. " And it contained an absurdity," was his later criticism.

Nor did he learn of the victory at Mans except through a pencilled note from the King. The staff had neglected to advise him of it. Bismarck bitterly complained, at various times, of this state of things. " Such ingratitude! " said he: " how can they treat me so, I, who have always defended the interests of the army in the Reichstag? but who lives shall see. I shall know how to change sides at need, and they will see the military enthusiast return to Germany a Parliamentarian; yes, I am quite capable of taking my seat with the extreme left!"

Hence, Bismarck's rage when Germany seemed to accuse him of prolonging unnecessarily the siege of Paris; him, who considered himself the humble victim of the military evasions and tergiversations. It is in fact well-known that Bismarck's one idea was to finish the bombardment as promptly as possible; so animated became the discussion of this point with the generals that he even threatened to resign.

At table Bismarck was unsparing in sarcasms levelled against the staff. He asserted that von Moltke was so possessed by the notion of war with France that, after the

Hohenzollern affair, he seemed to become rejuvenated or to age at sight according as events promised immediate war, or rendered the chances of it more remote.

General Steinmetz, in Bismarck's eyes, was but a shedder of blood. "At Gravelotte he really abused the enormous bravery of our troops," he said; and added, speaking of the battles fought under the walls of Metz: "The jealousy of our generals is the cause of our having lost so many men."

General von Budrizki, who, at Bourget, marched at the head of his troops, flag in hand, he sarcastically likened to the Belloir of the Berliners, an upholsterer and decorator named Hittl. "A general's place is not at the head of his troops," he concluded; "his mission is not decorative, but a *rôle* of surveillance and of direction."

Again at Ferrières, he said: "More than one of our generals abuse the self-abnegation of our soldiers by giving themselves the glory of a victory. After all, the hardened rascals of the staff are perhaps right when they say that if the 500,-000 men whom we have in France were destroyed, they would but represent our stakes; and it matters little if they are lost, provided the game is eventually won. To take the bull by the horns is an easy stratagem."

It is seen that Bismarck never missed an opportunity to criticise the operations of his rivals. He even denied them the merit of knowing enough to engage in battle upon a fixed date; remarking that the battle of Gravelotte, which should not have taken place until August 29th, had been fought merely at the will of the advance-guard.

Bismarck was evidently covetous of the part of a Blücher, even of a Napoleon. "Ah!" he exclaimed, "if I were an officer in perpetuity, as I would be, I should now be at the head of an army and we should not be before Paris."

At Commercy he had his own plan of campaign, which so impressed him that he confided it to the King, recommending it upon the childish pretext that it had succeeded in 1814. The plan was simply to have the cavalry light the way, on the march, and the infantry explore the ground to right and left. The most elementary notions of service in the country, it must be admitted; and the plan was not one to advance, in the minds of the German staff officers, Bismarck's strategic reputation. Yet the King approved it.

At Sedan, he it was who directed the conference relative to the capitulation, and the following is the relation of the proceedings made to his faithful Busch:

After the battle of the first of September I went to Donchéry with Marshal von Moltke to open negotiations with the French. There we spent the night, while the King returned to head-quarters at Vendresse. The conference lasted until after midnight without result. General Blumenthal and three or four staff officers took part in it, with von Moltke and me. General von Wimpfen spoke for the French. Marshal von Moltke simply stipulated that the entire French army should deliver itself up a prisoner. General von Wimpfen objected that it was too severe an exaction; the army had, by its bravery, earned a better fate. His chief, that it might be permitted to retire upon condition that, during the remainder of the campaign, it would not serve against us, and that it should be sent into Algeria or into any other French territory upon which we should determine.

Marshal von Moltke coldly repeated his conditions. General von Wimpfen represented his unfortunate position. Only two days since had he arrived from Africa and joined his troops; he had taken command only toward the end of the engagement, after Marshal MacMahon had been wounded; and now he was called upon to sign such a capitulation. Marshal von Moltke expressed his regret at being unable to take into consideration the General's position, which nevertheless he appreciated. He did homage to the valour of the French troops, but declared that they could not successfully defend Sedan, and that to pass through our lines was impossible. He asked nothing better than to have an *aide-de-camp* of the General visit our positions in order to convince himself of the fact.

General von Wimpfen then attacked the political side of the question; saying that from that view-point prudence advised us to accord him better conditions. We could not but desire a prompt and permanent peace, and of that we could not be assured unless we showed ourselves generous. By sparing the army we should win his gratitude and that of the entire nation, and awaken everywhere friendly sentiments. A contrary decision would mark the beginning of an interminable war.

Upon this I continued the discussion, because the reply to that argument lay within my domain: "The gratitude of a prince may be counted upon," I said, "but not the gratitude of a people; and the gratitude of the French is more to be doubted than that of another people. Neither situations nor institutions endure in France. Dynasties and governments succeed each other without intermission; and the one naturally is not bound by the promises made by the other. Since this state of things obtains we should be foolish not to follow up our success. The French are an envious and jealous people. The victory of Kœnigsgrœtz wounded them and they have never pardoned it, although it took nothing from them. How is our generosity going to make them forget Sedan?"

General von Wimpfen did not yield; he insisted that the French character had been modified by time and events. "France," said he, "learned under the Empire to regard peace as of more importance than military glory; she is ready to proclaim the fraternity of the nations," etc., etc. It was easy for me to prove to him the contrary and to show him that to grant his demand would but prolong the war indefinitely. I concluded by saying that our demands must be insisted upon.

General Castelnau then spoke, declaring in the name of his Sovereign that the Emperor had the day before given up his sword to the King only in the hope of obtaining honorable terms of capitulation. "What sword was it?" I asked, "the sword of France or the Emperor's own?" "The Emperor's sword," was the reply. "Then," exclaimed Marshal von Moltke, "there can be no question of other conditions," and a smile of satisfaction brightened his face. "Good," said General Wimpfen; "in that case we shall fight once more to-morrow." "I shall open fire at four o'clock," replied Marshal von Moltke. The French moved as if to go but I persuaded them to remain and think twice upon the matter. They finally decided to ask for an extension of the armistice that they might have time to consult with their colleagues at Sedan regarding our demands. Marshal von Moltke was at first unwilling to consent to it but I represented that a prolongation of the truce would not in any way injure our interests, and he yielded.

On the second, at six o'clock in the morning, General Reille came to my lodging in Donchéry and said the Emperor desired to speak with me. I dressed and mounted my horse to ride to Sedan where I expected to find him; but he was met at Fresnais, three kilometres from Donchéry, beside the pavement. He was seated, with three of his officers, in a carriage drawn by two horses, and three more officers accompanied the carriage. I recognized only MM. Reille, Castelnau, de la Moskowa and Joubert. I had stuck my revolver through my sash and the Emperor's eyes were fastened upon it for a full minute.

Here followed a remark unflattering, no doubt, to Napoleon; an expression, at any rate, so undiplomatic that Busch thought it necessary to excuse himself from repeating it. Bismarck continued:

I gave him the military salute; he took off his *képi* and the officers followed his example; I imitated them although it is contrary to our military rules. "Put on your cap," he said. I treated him precisely as I had at Saint Cloud and asked him what his orders were. He desired to speak to the King. I assured him that that was impossible, the King's head-quarters being two leagues distant. The fact is I did not wish him to see the King until the terms of the capitulation were settled. He next asked where he could stop, which indicated that he was averse to a return to Sedan.

Finally they rode down to Donchéry and, as the Emperor insisted upon seeing the King, Bismarck withdrew his objections and conducted him to the Château de Bellevue, near Fresnais, where the interview took place. " But," the Chancellor added, " it was arranged so that Napoleon could not see the King until after the conditions of the capitulation had been settled by von Moltke; military men being always more severe in such questions."

In the course of this brilliant march through France, pillaged, burned, despoiled, Bismarck found opportunity to remark that the French peasants were still as invariably ugly as when he was here in his diplomatic character. " I cannot understand it! " he protested to Busch, " one must conclude that the pretty ones go to Paris to invest their capital."

The humorist finally awoke; the humorist whose *bon mots* Busch collected at Versailles; the humorist whose fancy is at its best only when he writes. In his table-talk he is rather heavy and his jests are nearly always in deplorably bad taste, as will be seen in the following chapter. I will terminate this one with an anecdote full of genuine humour, the honour of which, however, belongs to a simple Prussian soldier who succeeded in outdoing the Chancellor.

Bismarck was ordered by the King to present a cross to a Bavarian gunner whose heroism was the cause of his being severely wounded. He sought the modest foot-soldier with the full intention of serving the man one of his characteristic turns.

" I am charged by the King," said Bismarck, " to bestow upon you this cross, or instead of it the sum of one hundred *thalers;* whichever you may choose."

The poor fellow, for the moment disconcerted, looked at the Chancellor who continued imperturbably serious. Then, his determination taken, he resolutely asked:

" How much is the cross worth? "

" About seventy-five *thalers*," replied Bismarck.

The man reflected a moment, then said ingenuously:

"Well, give it to me and twenty-five *thalers* to boot; that will even the account."

The Chancellor complied, confessed himself beaten and went off to relate the incident to the King, whom it greatly amused.

The Bismarck Arms.

VII.

The Chancery of the Confederation at Versailles—Discussions and Conferences Upon Gastronomy—A *Mot* of Arsène Houssaye—Bacchic Exploits of Bismarck—Berlin Wit—The *Menu* of *Foreign Affairs*—A Well-Guarded House—National Industry of Prussia—The Factory at Versailles and Its Head—Ingenuity of a Prussian Correspondent—How History is Written—Bismarck in His Dressing-Gown—The "Varieties" of the "Berlin Novelist."

After the decisive victories which have been mentioned the Prussians invested Paris. They established their headquarters at Versailles and Bismarck was installed at the hôtel of Mme. Jessé, Rue de Provence, No. 12; there was then an end of indifferent food and lodging. The table became the object of the peculiar care of his associates. "Their culinary artist, a simple soldier, served them breakfasts and dinners to which one accustomed to the plain *cuisine bourgeoise* must render this justice," said Mr. Busch, "he transported them into the bosom of Abraham; particularly because, among other celestial gifts, the gentlemen enjoyed exquisite wines and champagne at every meal!"

As a rule the repasts were seasoned with *bon mots*, jests and political and gastronomical discussions which the historiographer Busch has faithfully recorded.

At Ferrières, in the sumptuous dining-room of the Rothchilds' château, Bismarck entered upon an endless dissertation upon fish as a dish for the table, during which he found occasion to praise the superb trout in his lakes at Varzin. He also remarked by-the-way, that he was very fond of salted herring; happily for him, because that passion some years later saved his life, as will be seen in the section of this book devoted to Friedrichsruh.

He is fond of oysters, especially of broiled oysters; a preference which, to our thinking, constitutes a crime of lèse-gastronomy. Someone having mentioned mushrooms, the Chancellor seized the opportunity to prove that the countryman was not dead in him, and named in detail all the species of mushrooms to be found in the north. A peroration upon fruits crowned the discourse, when he declared himself a devout *amateur* in the cultivation of cherries, plums, of wild fruits even more particularly; such as blackberries and blueberries, which are plentiful in Germany.

Another day, wines, beers, liquors, were discussed. Although Bismarck is himself a beer-drinker he deplored the abuse of it in Germany, saying that it made one stupid, lazy, impotent, and was besides the source of all the political gossip at the grog-shops. This, certainly, was a judgment hardly flattering to the Chancellor's compatriots. As for him, he said, he held to the Prussian dictum: " Red wines for children, champagne for men and ' schnapps ' [brandy] for generals." Brandy is, as a matter of fact, the alcoholic stimulant which Bismarck prefers to all others; without prejudice to the Rhenish wines and champagne, porter or even tea and sherry—which von Moltke drank at Ferrières.

With such principles it was hardly astonishing that the Chancellor should and did occasionally sacrifice his time to the indulgence of his intemperate inclinations; he did not seek to dissemble the weakness—which is shared by the greater number of Germans: on the contrary! he gloried in it, complacently recalling the Bacchic prowess of which he had given proof in his younger days, and proudly remarking that his head resisted admirably the most formidable bumpers. Given a little encouragement, he would have posed as the father of diplomatic intemperance, yet Talleyrand surpassed him in like exploits.

Arsène Houssaye used to assert that champagne was the sovereign remedy for all ills, and that a *tisane de champagne* was the best of medicinal *tisanes*. Bismarck holds precisely the same opinion; he has used this remedy many times when excessively fatigued and always with most satisfactory results. Upon one occasion, in the course of a hunt, the officers of a regiment whom they chanced to visit offered a banquet to the King and his suite. Bismarck was presented with an enormous goblet in the form of a barrel, filled to the brim with champagne, the officers rejoicing in advance at the idea of fuddling the diplomatist. Bismarck, however, tranquilly accepted the proffered goblet, held his breath and drained it at a gulp; then, to the consternation of the officers, he requested another and would have emptied it in the same manner had not the King interposed.

But these gastronomical dissertations are not the only ones reported by Herr Busch. The German Macchiavelli touched upon all subjects with his rather heavily humorous appreciation. Often, after a bottle of old Pommard, would one catch the word " cruel " followed by many gallophobic prophecies.

Bismarck would sometimes imagine, as a consequence of the victories which he anticipated, " the transformation of a part of France into a German colony of eight or ten million souls; a kind of neutral territory, without an army, upon which Germany would be satisfied merely to levy taxes." Sometimes purely humorous impressions composed the conversation; the master depicted the state of his mind during his conference with Napoleon III., a prisoner, in the woodcutter's hut at Donchéry; saying that he felt upon that occasion much the sensation which must be experienced by a dancer at a ball who, having asked a young girl to dance the cotillion with him, finds nothing further to say and wishes himself well out of it.

At that same period Bismarck pronounced more or less absurd opinions concerning the " genius " of the French people. " Scratch a Frenchman," he said, " and you find a Turk." And again: " The French nation is only a crowd;

Villa Hollandia at Gastein, Habitation of Bismarck.

it lacks individuality, counts only *en masse*. There are in France thirty millions of obedient creatures who are individually valueless. It was easy to make of these creatures, lacking both character and personality, a force capable of destroying all in its path so long as our unity was not accomplished."

"Parisians, with their political superstitions, form a race apart, in France; they are narrow in their conceptions, which to them are sacred traditions, but which, closely examined, are found to be but hollow phrases, simply props."

When he saw Jules Favre again, four months after the conference at Ferrières, he thought him looking more grey and more stout, and remarked that the diet of horse-flesh had doubtless contributed to that result. Also when Jules Favre complained that the Germans had fired upon the *hospice des Quinze-vingts*, he replied:

"Why not? The French fired upon our men, who were well and vigorous."

Another time, Jules Favre having said that at Paris the women were to be seen walking on the boulevards with very pretty, healthy-looking children, Bismarck, pretending surprise, exclaimed: "You astonish me! I supposed you had eaten them all."

A propos of the French peasants who, by way of reprisal, were burned in their cabins, Bismarck declared the odour was "like that of roasted onions."

To the Prince Royal whom Bismarck invited to his table, and who was enthusiastic over the *menu*, he smilingly remarked that they were the specialties of foreign affairs.

"The inhabitants of the Confederation of the North," he added, "absolutely insist upon having a fat chancellor."

To Mme. Jessé, the proprietor of the hôtel in the Rue de Provence, he remarked upon taking his leave that he would with pleasure have eaten some of the eggs laid by her Guinea-hens but that, through patriotism no doubt, they had obstinately refused to lay while he was in the house.

From M. Delerot's book, "Versailles pendant l'occupation," we borrow some lines concerning the appearance of that house which was for some months "The diplomatic centre of Europe." (Herr Busch emphatically called it "the centre of civilized Europe.")

Placed in a street sufficiently retired and easy of surveillance, surrounded by a large garden and completely isolated from the neighbouring houses, this mansion offered exceptional conditions of security, which Herr von Bismarck seems to have sought before all else. As an added precaution, all the surrounding houses were occupied by agents of

The Château of Varzin.

the Chancellor. The house upon the other side of the street remained vacant; that adjoining had some narrow windows opening upon the hôtel Jessé; the proprietors were requested to close these windows with boards and to receive, as a guest, a detective. In a word, the entire street, having become exclusively the domain of the Chancellor, was inaccessible to anyone having hostile designs.

All day a police officer patrolled the street; night and day sentinels guarded the door of the hôtel. From the moment of his arrival Herr von Bismarck was preoccupied with the protection of the future Chancellor of the German Empire from the dangers to which he knew him to be exposed from the French or from the Germans themselves. At the grill of the hôter Jessé was a soiled white cotton banner bearing the following inscription in German: "Chancellor's Office of the Confederation." This banner was simply attached to the trunk of a tree still covered with its bark. In this, as in many other cases, if no necessary precautions were omitted to insure safety, no sacrifices were made to appearances.

The saying of Mirabeau is well known: "War is the national industry of Prussia." Bismarck at Versailles was himself the very soul of this industry; organizing, watching all, condescending to the very smallest details of military management; directing not only the home—or main—manufactory of the hôtel Jessé but even the branch establishments in Berlin.

The almost superhuman facility, according to Herr Busch, with which the Chancellor executed every work of creation, of assimilation or of criticism; accomplished the most difficult tasks, knew instantly the real solution of matters, was never so admirable as during that period; and that aptitude, which seemed inexhaustible, was the more surprising because he did not have sufficient sleep to make up the loss of vitality dispensed in such exceptional activity.

As a matter of fact we have already spoken of his frequent insomnia and of the banal causes to which one is tempted to attribute it; yet as he has himself confessed upon this subject it would be ungracious in us further to insist. Retiring very late, the Chancellor rose late—toward ten o'clock, generally, even in the country, unless a battle were planned, as the battles ordinarily were, to begin at day-break. At Versailles hardly was he out of bed, often before dressing, when he began to read, to take notes, to question his collaborators and to assign them their work. Then he took a cup of tea, an egg or two, and began to write or to dictate. He then ate no

The Old Emperor and his Chancellor.

more until evening; taking tea again between nine and ten o'clock.

In the afternoon he received visits, granted audiences, made his report to the King and attended to the expedition of telegrams and communications to the press. About two or three o'clock, however, he snatched a moment to breathe, to rest, to go out on horseback; then returning to work, he remained at it until the dinner-hour, which was between five and six o'clock. He left the table to continue his tasks, and for this reason dinner was to him the only agreeable hour of the day; a period of expansion, of mental freedom, when the natural man, inclined to absurd sallies, to jests a trifle brutal, mingled with amiable *witz* and coarse raillery, claimed all his rights.

At midnight the factory was closed and all the fires extinguished, but the master lingered later still, forging some new logomachical arm, replenishing in the bosom of night and of silence his provision of diplomatic " iron and fire."

Not a despatch, not a correspondence, not an article was there which did not fall under his eyes. And unhappy the secretaries or journalists who had the mischance to commit errors or print truths of a nature to displease him. At Clermont-en-Argonne he did not hesitate to suppress the correspondence of Louis Schneider, the historiographer and prime favorite of the King, accused and proved to have displayed too much zeal. The incident is worthy of relation and we leave its reporting to the German publicist himself.

Chance would have it that I should encounter in the street at Clermont, Count von Bismarck; he addressed me with his usual candour, telling me that there had been complaint at Berlin of the inexactitude of which I had been guilty. In consequence he had ordered that no more articles should be received from the same correspondent and it was impossible for him to revoke the order. Had he known it was I whom it would affect, he might not have taken the step; but what was done, was done, and must take its course. The matter might easily be arranged, however, if I would consent to submit my correspondence to an officer of the staff, who would inspect it.

The journalist at first accepted this condition but was not long in recognizing that his task was thereby rendered impossible; his correspondence, thus retarded, when it finally reached its destination was found to have been superseded by special letters from untrammeled reporters; his own letters were therefore valueless. "Besides," he observed, "when one must think of the censor one becomes cold and colorless; *it is, too, an undertaking almost impossible to one who has any regard for his dignity.*"

Upon the heels of this avowal the good German added, with an ingenuousness which makes one's hair rise and starts the goose-flesh:

"In spite of all, I acquitted myself zealously of my duty, copying each article clearly, to be submitted to the examiner."

Now that we have seen the unction with which Bismarck regulated the correspondence of the press let us listen to the Chancellor's appreciation of the same proceeding when he had reason to suppose it indulged in by the enemy:

I have always blamed the system of false news or press lies, of which the Empire made so much use and of which your Republic continues to make use (thus to the Mayor of Versailles). Of this statement I can furnish you a proof— the occasion, a combat which lately took place at Hay. I have the reports and official pieces upon the losses experienced; in a certain space upon the battle-field, where the projectiles from your fortifications fell, our troops buried the dead, French and Germans; there were more than four hundred and fifty French dead and eighty-five Germans. That is perfectly comprehensible; our troops, being sheltered, fired from behind crenelated walls, while your soldiers were entirely exposed. I do not mention now the loss which our artillery, of which the exactness of aim is well known, inflicted upon your men; it is supposed, at least, to equal the above in number; we have not been able to verify it, because the most distant corps to be reached fell too near to your fortifications to be recovered. We may then, say; nine hundred French killed, against eighty-five Germans. Well! your journals said: " About four hundred French killed and wounded, against more than five hundred Germans."

This declaration now appears the more ridiculous that we know by official documents, published in Germany itself, that the estimate of the Germans' loss at Hay was in reality four hundred men.

We owe to the author of " Versailles pendant l'occupation," already cited, a very curious portrait of Bismarck in *robe de chambre*, in which the Colonel of cuirassiers and his principal attributes disappear under the folds of the material like the furniture in a provincial *salon*.

Count von Bismarck was seated before a table which formed a desk, and was covered with a mass of papers among which were recent letters and journals from Paris. He was enveloped in a large dressing-gown of silk, and at the conclusion of the interview he excused himself for the negligence of his attire. The dressing-gown was worn over a military uniform. Upon the mantel was a helmet swathed in a kind of article like a furniture cover; this Herr von Bismarck lifted from time to time. Upon a commode lay a revolver. This environment had somewhat the air of being affected to show the alliance of the soldier and the diplomatist.

It is just to add that Bismarck was prostrated by an attack of gout, which contributed not a little to spoil for him the end of the campaign.

His double *rôle* of diplomatist and soldier in no wise interfered with his solicitude concerning the Berlin gazettes. With the intention, doubtless, of stanching the wounds which he might make, in acting rigorously against the zeal of their correspondents, he willingly furnished them with copy. In the course of one of his interviews with the Mayor of Versailles, he said:

"The point to which the Imperial Government pushed corruption is incredible. Documents found at the Tuileries are most edifying as bearing out that fact; some of the leaders of the democratic party are terribly compromised; it will be necessary to expose them in our little journal."

And in fact the " Nouvelliste de Berlin," which inserted a number of articles emanating from the Chancellor's residence, published *en variétés* during several weeks extracts from papers stolen from the Tuileries.

VIII

The Journal of Count d'Hérisson—Bismarck Overwhelmed with Praise—Count d'Hérisson Mistakes Bladders for Lanterns—More Table-Talk—Bismarck and Rothschild's Major-Domo—A Little Impartiality, if You Please—Theory upon Cigars—Bismarck and Garibaldi — A Witty, but Vague, Gesture — The Chancellor's Little Christmas—The Diplomatist's Decorations—The Prussians Quit Versailles—Mme. Jessé's Poultry—The Romance of a Clock—Deceptive Parallel Between Stage " Properties " and Historical Decorations—Bucolic—Bismarck Pronounces the Final Word.

In the house of Mme. Jessé took place all the conferences relative to the armistice. Jules Favre, who negotiated the peace with Count von Bismarck, was habitually accompanied by an officer of the Staff, M. le Comte d'Hérisson.

The latter, who was once invited to Bismarck's table, has left in his "Journal of an Ordonnance Officer," some very curious impressions which are worthy of being related.

The appreciation of M. d'Hérisson concerning Bismarck's attitude and proceedings at Versailles are inclined to be eulogistic; too much so, in our opinion, coming from a French officer.

After our preface we can hardly be suspected of chauvinism; we believe also in moderation in all things, and in unduly exalting such a man as Bismarck there is risk of winning his contempt and of misleading public opinion.

M. d'Hérisson begins by saying:

Were three-quarters-and-a-half of the French publications, the journals and the public opinion formed by them relative to the war to be believed, Count von Bismarck, the

Chancellor of Prussia, must be not only a kind of Richelieu, under whose will all bent, who commanded and was accountable to none for his conduct, but Bismarck must be a man of iron; determined to win every success; to exhaust victory; who had planned our fall and his own demands in advance; whom nothing arrested, who cared no more for the rest of Europe than for a cherry; who, in a word, knew how far he might go and would not stop until he had reached that point. Nothing is more untrue than this conception.

Count Herbert von Bismarck, Elder Son of the Chancellor.

No doubt; but, also, nothing is more untrue than the contrary conception, which is that of M. d'Hérisson, by whom Bismarck is represented as a man whose religion and patriotism dictated an exceptional moderation corroborated by his lively desire to cut short as promptly as possible the evils of the war, and that out of pure humanity.

First, Bismarck is not so religious as M. d'Hérisson believes. I know Herr Busch pretended to have found upon his night-table at Versailles pious books, which had doubtless been sent him by his wife; and the historiographer at another time relates that before leaving for the war the Chancellor took communion; but that proves nothing.

For Bismarck religion is before all an affair of sentiment; and one of his own principles is not to confuse sentiment and concerns of the war. "In the matter of war," he has many times declared, "one must ask one's self whether one has or has not an interest in crushing one's adversary."

Now Germany undoubtedly had an interest in crushing France, but not at its own expense. The chances of a mortal, an excessive war are occasionally deceptive and Bismarck knew that in the eyes of the German nation he alone would be held responsible for all the German blood spilled. For that reason was his attitude conciliatory, his care constant to spare the life of the simplest Prussian soldier, his fervent desire to end it at any price; that, the cause of the fury into which he was thrown by the resistance of Paris and later by the dilatoriness of Jules Favre and Thiers.

That is not humanity, it is diplomacy.

M. d'Hérisson seems to have imperfectly comprehended him, and he takes in good faith replies like the following, which Bismarck opposed to an apostrophe by Jules Favre, asking him if he did not fear to exasperate the resistance of the Parisians.

"Ah, you talk of your resistance! you are proud of your resistance! Very well, Monsieur, know that if M. Trochu were a German general I should have him shot this evening. One has not the right, do you hear? one has not the right, in the face of humanity, in the face of God, for a vain military aureole, to expose to the horrors of famine as he is this moment doing, a city of two million souls. The railway lines are everywhere cut. If we be unable to re-establish them in two days, and it is uncertain that we shall be able, a hundred thousand women in Paris will die daily of starvation. Do not talk of your resistance—it is criminal!"

They had begun that day with the discussion of the figure to be contributed for the war. Bismarck laughingly declared that Paris was such a "*grande dame,*" such an opulent person, that it would be insulting to demand less than a milliard; nevertheless he consented to fix the sum at 200,000,000 francs.

The dinner-hour arrived and covers had been laid for these gentlemen at the Chancellor's table. Jules Favre declined the honour; our captain, who had not the same scruples, took his place with a dozen gilded and embroidered Prussians who were habitual guests of the master.

He, who sat in the middle of the table, seated the French officer at his right:

I remember, says M. d'Hérisson in his "Journal," that the table, which was well served and garnished with the necessary quantity of massive silver, was lighted by only two candles, stuck into the necks of empty bottles. Only this detail, possibly calculated, recalled the campaign.

Hardly was the Chancellor seated when he began to eat with a good appetite, the while chatting and drinking quantities, alternately, of beer and champagne, from a huge silver drinking-cup engraved with his cipher.

All talked French.

The conversation suddenly became most animated. According to his custom Bismarck, *en passant*, launched a few sharp remarks principally at the proprietor of Ferrières, or rather at his intendant and at Jews in general, for whom the Chancellor expresses but an indifferent esteem.

Here let us, parenthetically, explain the motive of the rancour which he nourished against Rothschild and Rothschild's major-domo during his sojourn. At the Château de Ferrières the major-domo had refused to give out any wine, although assured that the requisitions were paid.

Summoned before the Chancellor he began by saying that

he had none, and ended by admitting that the cellars held some *petit bordeaux*. Bismarck, furious, replied that so ill-taught a person as he was much out of place in a *château* which the King honoured with his presence and his protection. Then, suddenly:

"Do you know," he added, what a *strohbund* is?" " As the poor fellow could not guess, it was explained that a *strohbund* is a bundle of straw upon which it sometimes happens in Germany that recalcitrant stewards are laid, with the back uppermost. The rest goes without saying.

The unhappy man understood, of course, for from that day Bismarck's table no longer lacked wine.

After dinner Count d'Hérisson, by his own admission, deployed all the seduction of his *esprit boulevardier* and succeeded in pleasing the terrible cuirassier-diplomat whom it was necessary to propitiate as far as possible; the conference with Jules Favre was continued. The negotiations were re-opened sedately, gently.

With astonishing candour and admirable logic the Chancellor explained simply and sincerely his desires. He went always straight to the point, at every point disconcerting Jules Favre, accustomed as an advocate to *finesse*, to diplomatic jobbing, and not in the least understanding the perfect loyalty, the superb manner, little conformable to the old digressive fashion of treating such matters.

The Chancellor expressed himself in French with a facility which I have rarely found equalled even among the Russians, who so promptly and felicitously assimilate our language, and to whom the difficulties of their own render the study of foreign idioms only child's-play. He used expressions at once forceful and elegant, finding without seeking and without effort the proper words in which to clothe his thought or define a situation.

While drawing the pieces as they were needed from the ministerial portfolio, and writing the notes as they were dictated to me, I regaled myself with this unexpected lesson in rhetoric and conversation.

It is singular that in this report, written by an officer of the French staff, it was Bismarck who had the noble part against Jules Favre, described as an artful dodger and a jobber.

The lesson in rhetoric with which the Count d'Hérisson was regaled began by the expounding of a subtile theory upon the cigar and upon smoking in general. Bismarck had offered Jules Favre Havana cigars, which he declined. The Chancellor then said:

"You are wrong. When a conversation is begun which may lead to discussion, engender violence of language, it is better to smoke while talking. When one smokes, you see," he continued, lighting the Havana, "this cigar which one holds and fingers and is careful not to let fall, a little paralyzes the physical movements. Morally, without depriving us of our mental faculties, it soothes us. The cigar is a' diversion; this blue smoke which mounts in rings and which the eyes involuntarily follow, charms one into a more conciliatory mood. One is happy, the sight is occupied, the hand restrained, the sense of smell satisfied. There is a disposition to mutual concession; and the duty of us diplomats is comprised in reciprocal and incessant concession. You have, you who do not smoke, over me, a smoker, this advantage: you are more wide awake; and a disadvantage: you are more inclined to fly off at a tangent, to yield to the first impulse," he pursued with a suspicion of irony.

Very pretty, truly, these aphorisms of a confirmed smoker and a man with an excellent digestion; unhappily Bismarck disproved the conclusion of his principles five minutes later by boiling over like a milk porridge *à propos* of Garibaldi, whom he would exclude from the peace that he might revenge himself upon Italian ingratitude.

"The Chancellor's eyes," said the Count d'Hérisson, "suddenly flamed with savage anger."

"I must take him, nevertheless," he exclaimed; "for I

intend to march him through Berlin with a placard inscribed: 'This is Italian gratitude.' What! after all we have done for those people? it is monstrous!"

At that moment the Count d'Hérisson had a genial idea.

I then permitted myself a rather bold thing, but which, toward a man of distinction and especially of education like Bismarck, had a chance of success, and did, in fact, succeed. I took the cigar holder and half smiling, half bending in an attitude of respectful supplication, I offered it to him. For a few seconds he did not understand, then the flame of wrath died out of his eyes: "You are right, Captain," he said, "it is useless to be angry; that serves nothing—on the contrary!"

Garibaldi and his little army were from that time included in the armistice, and we can but felicitate Jules Favre upon an insistence which was well justified by the devotion of the patriotic Italian.

Until the cessation of hostilities the *usine* at Versailles preserved, within and without, its air of tranquil provincialism; except upon the occasion of Christmas, which Bismarck, as a good German, could not refrain from celebrating. The traditional pine-tree, decorated with toys and candles, was erected in one of the chambers of the Chancellor's residence and the entire household, including the domestics, the porter and his children, were invited to take part in the *fête*, during which there was an abundant distribution of toys and cigars. Bismarck himself had received his little remembrance, the King his master having just conferred upon him the order of the Iron Cross.

This Iron Cross was the only decoration which he afterward wore, as he had worn in the Chamber at Berlin only the modest badge for heroism, presented to him for having saved his domestic, Hildebrand, from drowning. It is even reported that one of the members of Parliament, greatly concerned as to the possible significance of the badge, upon questioning Bismarck, received the reply:

"What would you? every one has his caprices; mine is to occasionally save a man's life."

The German biographers recount *à propos* of Bismarck a less pacific incident regarding his later diplomatic decorations.

The Château of Friedrichsruh.

In the course of a military review which took place at Frankfort during the Diet (1854), Bismarck, for once departing from his invariable custom, adorned his cuirassier's uniform with all his diplomatic stars and other orders. An Austrian general approaching him, asked if he had won all those decorations before the enemy.

Whether the question was an intentional sarcasm or

Field-Marshal von Moltke.

simple ingenuousness is not known; but it displeased Bismarck, who, looking the Austrian straight in the eyes, coldly replied:

"Yes, Excellency, all before the enemy, here, in Frankfort."

The preliminaries of the peace signed, the Chancellor's residence was laboriously prepared for the departure of the household. Here I borrow for the last time from the book of M. Delerot, facts noted the same day from the relation of witnesses—principally Mme. Jessé;—facts which later stories have somewhat distorted. On the evening before the departure of Bismarck, March 5th, having sent for Mme. Jessé he insisted upon her inspection of the hôtel in order that she might convince herself of the care he had taken to preserve the furniture, etc., from all possible injury.

"I have respected even your poultry, although they have annoyed me greatly at times." Yet upon seeking diligently no fowls were to be discovered; the cook was finally obliged to acknowledge that his Excellency had had them all served at table.

The tour of inspection continued, accompanied by observations by turn jesting and obsequious from Bismarck. Mme. Jessé next missed from its place a marble clock, surmounted by a bronze statuette of a winged Satan. Bismarck replied that he had had it removed to his office.

"Thiers detested that clock," he continued, "we always argued before it, and at last he exclaimed: 'That devil! that cursed devil!' yet it was under the wings of that same devil that we signed the peace. By-the-way, do you greatly value the clock?"

Mme. Jessé having replied in the affirmative Bismarck said no more. The visit of inspection at an end he courteously reconducted his landlady to the Boulevard de la Reine.

Mme. Jessé had almost reached the Lycée when two

horsemen joined her; one of them dismounting, said to her, (here I quote M. Delerot):

"Madame, that clock which Herr von Bismarck mentioned to you, it would give us great pleasure to offer to him. His Excellency desires very much to take it with him as a souvenir. Will you let us have it? whatever the price, provided it be not a million," they added, smiling, " we will pay it."

Count von Hohenlohe.

Mme. Jessé refused and drove on to the railway station.

The request was repeated the following day by the Secretaries of the Count, but Mme. Jessé declined still more decidedly to part with the historic clock. " I am French," she said, " I will neither give it nor sell it."

Toward nine o'clock Herr von Bismarck appeared before the hôtel to enter his traveling-carriage. Mme. Jessé was standing near but he pretended not to see her. He bade the gardener farewell, leaving in the man's hand as he grasped it, fifty francs, adding afterward forty more with the direction to use the latter sum for necessary repairs to the hôtel and remarking that Mme. Jessé should be satisfied therewith.

The persons present were not sufficiently politic to dissimulate their relief at his departure, and Herr von Bismarck, glancing round him said in a tone half irritated, half ironical:

"How delighted everyone here is to see me show my heels!"

As to the clock, it remained in its place, but still preoccupied Herr von Bismarck's thoughts, for at the last moment he gave the gardener a scrap of paper, upon which was written his Berlin address, saying:

"If Mme. Jessé change her mind here is my address."

Shortly after Bismarck had gone Mme. Jessé discovered that from a secretary placed in the private office of Herr von Bismarck, to which none but the superior officers had access and where the armistice was signed, had been taken a rouleau of four hundred francs in gold, some jewels and a collection of rare money. Further, it was perceived that, if the clock was still there the pendulum had been detached; this had doubtless been done at the last moment by one of Bismarck's officers. Being unable to offer his master the clock itself he had perhaps wished at least to give him the pendulum which had marked those seconds which M. Thiers had so justly cursed.

The clock, deprived of its pendulum, still marks the hour at which Bismarck quitted Versailles.

As a scrupulously exact historian I considered it my duty to visit Mme. Jessé's hôtel, which, properly restored, bears the number 20—Rue de Provence. I was received by Mme. Jessé's own son, a severe young man who appeared much more interested in the cultivation of his garden than in contributing to the impartial examination of the historic souvenirs which had fallen into his possession. He is one of those people who forget each page of existence as the leaf is turned and readily believe that all their contemporaries share their own disdain of history. M. Jessé assured us that there existed in his house no trace of Bismarck's occupation. The furniture had been entirely replaced by new; except, indeed, the famous clock, which was still there, but which did *not* mark the historic hour as indicated by M. Delerot; which proves that there are in histories as in theatres, decorations which should not be too closely examined.

We have just passed in review the principal attitudes of Bismarck as a warrior. Herr Busch shows us the great master of the *usine* at Versailles, possessed, in spite of himself, by bucolic dreams to which he gave expression as follows:

"I had last night for the first time in a long while two good hours of sleep. Generally I lie awake, my brain assailed by all sorts of disquieting thoughts; then Varzin suddenly presents itself with perfect distinctness, even to the minutest details, as a vast landscape in colour; green trees with the sun shining athwart their trunks, the blue sky overhead and each tree standing out separately. It seems impossible, in spite of all my efforts, to escape from this obsession until it is dislodged by notes, reports, despatches, etc., and finally by sleep at day-dawn."

Bismarck's also is this final word upon the inhabitants of the *banlieu* returning to their homes after the capitulation of Paris.

"On my way to Saint Cloud to-day," he said at table, "I met a number of people carrying household utensils and bedding. The women looked amiable enough, but the men, when they saw our uniforms, assumed a gloomy air and an heroic pose. They recalled to me the fact that formerly in the Neapolitan army there was a singular regulation. Here we say: 'Arms to the right, for attack'; the Neapolitans say: '*Faccia feroce!*' With the French all is pompous, imposing, theatrical."

And this same man, gifted with so clear a perception of the weaknesses of others, never realized that he, a simple diplomatist, covered himself with ridicule by masquerading as a military man; wearing throughout the campaign in France a pointed helmet and top-boots, and not consenting to don his civilian's dress until the day following the signing of the peace preliminaries.

Always the history of the beam and the mote!

Medal Struck for the Eightieth Anniversary of Bismarck's Birth.

IX.

Bismarck, Landed Proprietor—Friedrichsruh—The Chancellor's Skepticism—His Literary Opinions and Preferences—Bismarck, Orator—His Tactics at the Sittings of the *Reichstag*—Eloquence and Alcoholism—A *Mot* About Alsace-Lorraine—"*Je crains Dieu, cher Abner, et n'a point d'autre crainte*"—Might Makes Right.

By the end of the year 1871 Bismarck, elevated to the rank of prince, had arrived at the apogee of his political career, and it may be imagined that he felt some pride in measuring the steps by which he had advanced since 1866. The Chancellor of the new German Empire was, in spite of his political enemies, the most universally adulated of any man in Germany. At the same time he was one of the richest land-owners in the country, and to his domains of Schönhausen and Varzin—this last purchased with the million-and-a-half *francs* presented to him by the Emperor William for his participation in the Austrian war—he had recently added the estate of Friedrichsruh, which represents a capital of several millions previously deducted by the Emperor from the five milliards of France.

We owe it to truth to say that this grandeur does not dazzle the simple, nature-loving man; in order to be convinced of it one would do well to read the pen-picture of Bismarck drawn by his childhood's friend—John Lothrop Motley.

I extract the following passage from a letter addressed by Motley to his wife, dated July 25, 1872:

I was surprised to find him [Bismarck] little changed, in appearance, since 1864. He is somewhat more stout, his features are a trifle altered but no less expressive of energy than of old. Madame von Bismarck is still less changed in these fourteen years since I last saw her. Marie is a delicious young girl with curling hair and gray eyes; simple, modest, valiant of heart like her father and mother.

When we left the table Bismarck walked with me in the forest; a walk enlivened by his gay jests, his interesting re-

At Kissingen: Awaiting Bismarck's Appearance.

view of the terrible years just past. He spoke as one would of the simplest daily occurrences, without the least affectation.

In the evening there was a large number of people present, drinking tea, beer, Seltzer water, while Bismarck smoked his pipe. Formerly he smoked the strongest cigars; now, he tells me, he would not smoke another to save his life, so repulsive have they become to him.

Among other things he said that in his youth he had considered himself a very cautious man, but that he had always been firmly convinced that none controls his destiny and consequently that none is truly great and powerful. He could not restrain a smile when he heard vaunted his wisdom, his prescience and the power which he exercised over the world's destiny. A man in his situation, he said, is forced to decree for the neutral crowd which hesitates to prognosticate either rain or fine weather for the morrow: "It will rain to-morrow; or, the weather will be fine"; and to see to it that his predictions are realized. If he is right the world cries: "What wisdom! what a gift of prophecy!" if wrong, all the old women overwhelm him with their contempt. Therefore life has taught him modesty if it has taught him nothing else.

The years which followed count among the fullest of Bismarck's career, from the diplomatic as from the parliamentary view-point. It is the general opinion in Germany that Bismarck is not, properly speaking, an orator. He himself does not hesitate to admit that eloquence is not his *forte;* excusing his lack of it by remarking that an orator is before all else a poet, an artist, and that such qualities are incompatible with those which go to the making of a political character. Bismarck is in no sense artistic; he hardly likes music and is entirely indifferent to painting; only a fortuitous circumstance, which he relates in one of his private letters, induced him to visit, once, the art gallery in Berlin.

In literature Bismarck is familiar only with romance, which fact might almost pass for a proof of intellectual inferiority had not Bismarck declared that he read only for distraction, having no time to devote to books demanding thought. Before 1870 our diplomatist had a marked predilection for French fiction; for Feydeau and the two Dumas; he carried their books upon all his journeys, even during the campaign. The day before the battle of Sadowa he wrote his wife to send him some French novels; it really seemed that he could conceive of no other aliment for his imagination. Later, when the vogue of the realistic school was at its height, he became an enthusiastic admirer of Flaubert, Zola, de Goncourt, "because," he said, "they paint in a superior manner the corrupt manners of the French nation." An English writer who had the good fortune to interview the Chancellor at that time gives the result of the opportunity as follows:

He smoked all the time, inviting me to do likewise; and he poured beer frequently into a mug which stood beside him. Near at hand was a pile of yellow-covered French novels, and when we had finished speaking of the business which had procured me the audience, the Prince asked me what French romances I preferred; and thereupon launched into a dissertation upon French literature which convinced me that he knew whereof he spoke.
I was struck with the facility with which he accepted the pictures of the romance-writers, their most sombre delineations of the social life of France, as a faithful reproduction of the customs of the country. He believed French society corrupt to the marrow, and was incapable of rendering justice to any of the good qualities which distinguish the French. He asserted with his characteristic brusqueness that the French had always been inclined to bespatter themselves, and that writers like Dumas *fils* and Zola, when accused of going too far, always denied having exaggerated anything in their writings.
I replied that according to that manner of passing judgment, if it were necessary to estimate the English by certain sensational novels of their country one would have to believe English society a motley collection of thieves, counterfeiters and scamps.
To this Bismarck replied with the courtesy which distinguishes him: "As a matter-of-fact, thieving is the national vice of the English; but it does not produce atrophy of the race as does the propensity of the French for women."

A psychological or literary judgment supported by such arguments is too open to discussion to permit us to insist upon its correctness.

The inferiority of Bismarck as an orator explains why in the later years of his career the Chancellor pronounced few discourses and showed himself as seldom as possible at the *Reichstag*. In fact Bismarck was present only on the days when it was necessary to defend the fundamental principles of his policy; the one, for instance, of the septennial duration of the term of military service.

Since it is impossible to sketch Bismarck in the tribune, we will reproduce here some paragraphs of an article by Herr Th. Zolling, which appeared in the " *Neue freie Presse* " in 1887:

The Chancellor tranquilly permitted the representatives of the countries to speak; in the interval he swallowed an absolutely incredible quantity of water to which he added a few drops of cognac.

From time to time he trifled with his lorgnette and its antique case which lay before him; now and then raising the glass to his eye and regarding the members. This, however, did not prevent his listening attentively to the speeches or taking notes in pencil. Oh, that pencil! it was one such as one does not see every day. It was yellow and of astonishing length. I have been told that regularly after each session the pencils disappeared, carried off by the deputies, who gave them to their wives as relics of Bismarck. * * * The Chancellor made a sign to a domestic, and he brought a great black leather portfolio which he placed on his master's knees. Bismarck took from his pocket a bunch of keys, opened the portfolio and took from it two bundles of papers, one red, the others blue, containing all the important pieces; he chose one and placed it before him and looked at his watch; for the chatterer upon the platform had not finished and the Chancellor was growing impatient.

At last his turn came.

He rose slowly and one experienced a curiously overpowering sensation at sight of that Hercules rising above the table, so tall that his fingers did not touch it. His arms waved right and left and his hands, which alone betrayed his age, became more tremulous, seeking a support; they pulled nervously at his moustache, his ears, his garments, the iron cross which was the Chancellor's only decoration. Again, he drew out his handkerchief and noisily blew his nose.

Speaking of his voice the German journalist said:

One expects to hear a tone of thunder issuing from that enormous chest; instead, it is a very agreeable baritone; gentle at first and becoming stronger after a few sentences.

His tone is never solemn or pathetic; only, it would seem, an ordinary conversation addressed to the nearer deputies; rarely reaching so far as the legislators.

A stenographer of the *Reichstag*, who has published his memoirs, expresses a somewhat analogous opinion:

It cannot be said that Prince von Bismarck is an orator. It is astonishing to find that this huge man has a most ladylike voice; it is particularly weak when the Prince is suffering from a nervous affection. Upon such occasions it is scarcely audible and is frequently interrupted by a violent cough. Thereafter only detached sentences are heard; there is no longer a discourse; he is perfectly master of his words and I have an idea that the cough is useful in assisting him to collect his ideas and produce an effect.

He begins, for instance, with a rather coarse phrase, which it is expected will be followed by one still stronger; not at all! the little cough opportunely arrives and after it comes an expression which no one could possibly have anticipated. Here is an example which I give from memory:

" I am in the service of the Emperor. It is a matter of absolute indifference to me whether or not I shall perish in that service; and you, [a little spell of coughing] you are probably equally indifferent."

Everyone expected to hear launched a gross expression, but no, the little cough changed the course of his ideas.

The Deputy Richter (continues Herr Zolling), "the *bête noire* of Bismarck," mounted the platform in his turn. He resembles M. Emile Zola, with his unattractive physique but facile elocution and elegant diction.

During the speaking of the progressionist deputy Bismarck seemed to be a prey to some strong emotion. His face changed colour; at first very pale, he became crimson; his eyes appeared as if starting from his head, then their brilliance was quenched. His hands toyed convulsively with the pencil and from time to time he added some notes to those before him. Now and then he attempted to take part in the general hilarity, but his laugh sounded forced and strident.

Suddenly he sprang up, in the midst of the uproar caused by Richter's speech, and pulled at his coat-tails in order to make him descend from the platform; precisely as though he intended to go at the Deputy "hammer and tongs"; his chest heaved violently and he seemed to be making the most prodigious effort to respire.

But while he took an instant in which to measure his adversary, in that instant he became master of himself; his humour suddenly changed. His natural gaiety returned— a smile lighted his countenance; he had regained complete possession of himself and replied in a bantering manner to his adversary, endeavouring to turn his speech into ridicule; every shot was well-aimed, every blow told. The oratorical battle ended amid shouts of laughter.

Let us note in passing that during his occupation of the platform Bismarck poured for himself large portions of a mixture of cognac and water, carefully prepared by a group of friends and by Count Herbert. On the days of the long sessions the ministers themselves superintended that matter.

When the fluids were combined the mixture was tasted by each of the group; some found it too strong; quick! a little water was added; those who tasted of it after that addition considered it too weak; quick! a little cognac must be put to it; and the gentlemen were so conscientious about

The Artificer of German Unity.

the business that they did not remark the reiterated appeals of the Chancellor, who was signing to them that his glass had long been empty.

During the session of February 6, 1888, Bismarck drank, according to Herr von Blowitz's report, eighteen glasses of his favorite mixture.

Bismarck has a horror of grand oratorical effects; he does not like the orators themselves any better; "for," he has said, "the least fault of a man who speaks too easily is to speak too frequently and at too great length." All the Chancellor's biographers are obliged to admit that generally, instead of listening to Richter, as Herr Zolling has just said, Bismarck decamped, not to return until his implacable adversary had left the platform. The Chancellor, when reproached for this weakness, excused himself by the assurance that the personality and oratorical violence of Herr Richter affected him to the very core of his being; he found it impossible to overcome his distaste.

The truth is, we believe, that the faithful *âme de chien féodal* of the Chancellor could not tolerate that liberty should be so much as mentioned; the symbolic *Reichshund* feared to become mad and bite.

Did the deputies from Alsace-Lorraine complain of the exceptionally severe terms imposed upon the annexed provinces, terms which were a violation of the conscience and the rights of the people, Bismarck replied with his characteristic humour: "It was not to insure the happiness of Alsace-Lorraine that we annexed it. We were forced to break that point of Wissembourg which too deeply penetrated our skin, and precisely upon that Alsacian point exists a population which yields in nothing to the Gaul as a passionate fighter, and which honours us with a truly cordial hatred."

In short what remains of the political speeches of Bismarck is very little indeed, and it is ludicrous to see the German biographers make admiring mention of the oratorical effect which consists in launching from the platform this defiance in the face of Europe: "We Germans, we fear God, but nothing else in the world!" (February 6, 1888.) A rhodomontade which is but a vulgar paraphrase of the famous verse of Racine: *Je crains Dieu, cher Abner, et n'ai point d'autre crainte.*")

As to the well-known maxim: "Might makes right," which appeared in his speech of January 27, 1863, Bismarck has himself declined to father it, in the following terms:

The orator has said that I made use of the words: " Might makes right." I do not remember having employed such an expression. In spite of the manifestations of incredulity with which my denial is received, I appeal to your memory, which, if it be as sure as mine, will tell you that I expressed myself rather in the following manner: I counselled compromise, because without it there must be conflict, that conflict raised the question of power, and that, as the life of the State could not be imperilled, whichever possessed power would be under the necessity of using it. I did not insist that it was an advantage. I do not pretend to desire an impartial judgment from you; I wish only to rectify a misunderstanding of my words.

X.

Bismarck in 1874—The Chancellor's Palace at Berlin—Humorous Notes upon the French and Germans—A Parliamentary Evening in 1879—The Lion is Old—The Attempt at Kissingen—The von Arnim Affair—Family Events—A Letter from the Chancellor to the Brother of his Stable-Boy—Bismarck's 70th Anniversary—National Subscription—The Château of Schönhausen and the French Cannon—Some Original Gifts—Bismarck Weeps.

We owe to the pen of M. Maurice Jokaï, the Hungarian novelist, some notes concerning the Bismarck of 1874, whom the writer visited at the Chancellor's palace in Berlin:

Nothing is more simple and easy than to meet Prince von Bismarck. The palace is the least pretentious place upon the Wilhelmstrasse, and the door is not guarded by majestic Swisses armed with a mass of silver. One must ring—neither more nor less is needed. The antechamber is lighted by a single lamp upon a table. I crossed two *salons* before reaching the Chancellor's study, in which he receives his callers. The furnishing is very modest: in the corner is an iron bed, upon which was stretched a great Saint Bernard; near the window is an iron strong-box; in the middle of the room an immense desk, before which the Chancellor was seated.

He motioned me to a place upon the other side of the desk and opened a drawer from which he took a bunch of cigars and offered them to me. I thanked him, but I do not smoke. He himself never smokes a cigar, but confines himself entirely to his great meerschaum. At this moment a door opened and the Princess appeared accompanied by her daughter; they were going to a ball at Court and had come to take leave of the head of the family. Bismarck kissed them patriarchally, and charged his wife to present his respects to their Majesties.

In the course of that audience Bismarck expressed himself with his customary candour concerning the French: "The French are savages; take away the cook, the tailor and the hair-dresser and only the red-skin will be left." It would be curious to imagine what would remain of the Prussians after removing these same elements of civilization, including those who constitute its national industry according to Mirabeau.

It may be added that in the course of this same interview Bismarck showed hardly more tenderness toward a number of his compatriots who had emigrated to Russia—and elsewhere.

"I have frequently hunted in Russia," he said, "and have often heard repeated this proverb: 'If a Russian steals, he steals sufficient to last his own life; but if a German steals he takes enough for his children to have afterward.'" (Of which we had proof in 1871.) This is the moment at which to say a few words of the Parliamentary receptions and *frühschoppen* [morning chop] which are celebrated in the history of the political *cuisine* of the time. They were generally intimate reunions when the man of iron, unbending from the official formality of the Imperial Chancellor, became malleable; sought to win over the lukewarm and the hesitating by a kind of affable good fellowship.

The "*frühschoppen*" especially, offered such Platonic adversaries as Windhorst, a neutral territory whereon to dispute without pulling of noses; the keg of brown Bavarian beer about which they gathered finally succeeding in conciliating opinions the most divergent.

Of the same kind were the Parliamentary receptions which followed the intimate dinners, veritable tobacco parliaments, the Germans called them, which lasted late into the night, and at which Bismarck, as a humorist peculiarly well-broken to the gymnastics of familiar conversation, must have scored his most felicitous oratorical successes.

A German writer, Herr Fedor von Koppen, has described in detail one of those evenings—that of May 3, 1879, when Bismarck was his most seductive self. The Chancellor stood in the yellow *salon* to receive his guests. His two sons, Herbert and Wilhelm, aided him, when he was unassisted by the Princess and her daughter, the Countess Marie, who had become a woman distinguished for her intelligence and wit. The guests were then led into the large *salon*, where the candlelight lent a warmer tone to the severe furniture of the Renaissance and to the green and gold-leaved tapestry upon the walls. All the men were in evening dress. Those wearing uniforms constituted themselves squires of dames, following the device: "*Amour à la plus belle, honneur au plus vaillant*" (sic).

Bismarck took his place at a little ebony table and was soon surrounded by an enthusiastic audience of deputies and political men; and the Chancellor began to joke and chat with the joviality which is natural to him when with his intimates—touching upon one subject after another, mingling politics, sports, hunting adventures, etc. A subject particularly dear to him, and of which he was never weary, was his childhood and youth; his student's escapades, his duels and the number of days of incarceration to which he submitted at Göttingen.

Suddenly a detonation was heard from the adjoining room. All rushed in, to find that a guest had been imprudently handling a fire-arm which he was examining and it had exploded. No one was injured, although the ball had just grazed a deputy who was standing near. Bismarck was no sooner assured of this than, seizing a glass, he smilingly proposed a toast to the deputy who had so fortunately escaped "*the attack of chance.*"

The Deputy Windhorst was present at this reception and Bismarck was particularly amiable to his adversary. At

The Saw-mills at Varzin.

ten o'clock, as usual, the guests were served an abundant collation, while in a corner of the room, under some orange trees, were placed two casks of Munich beer (Franciscan brewery); Bismarck, who has never been known to resist an opportunity to pun, presented these casks in the following words: "Gentlemen, I especially recommend this brewing; since the wind has turned, concerning Rome, the Franciscans send me of their choicest." Such, in a few words, were the every-day incidents of a reception at Bismarck's, incidents which the comic journals of the day eagerly seized and commented upon.

As a matter of fact Bismarck was then the only great man among the Berliners, who swore only by him. His most in-

The Paper-mills at Varzin.

significant sayings and doings were important to them. Fanatics followed his slow-moving carriage. The people might chaff about the old, ill-varnished van and smile at the faded blue livery of the coachman, it was their Bismarck who was passing and they were only too happy to salute him with a " *hoch!* "

It is singular that while his popularity augmented, his political authority diminished.

The Opposition was beginning to strengthen in the *Reichstag*, and to undermine the foundation of the colossus of iron. This man, who was approaching his sixtieth year, saw by little and little his warmest political friends drifting away from him; even Maurice von Blankenburg and Thadden Thriglaff—and many more. "The lion is getting old," they said; "he is losing his teeth." A few years more and, aided by the accession of William II., they were able to pare his claws.

On July 13, 1874, Bismarck, who was at Kissingen, in Bavaria, to take the waters for his rheumatism, escaped almost miraculously the ball of one Kullmann, who pretended that he wished to punish in Bismarck the promoter of religious persecution in Germany. (After this attempt, the city of Kissingen raised to him an iron statue which was unveiled in 1877. Even to the present time the ex-Chancellor has continued his annual visits to Kissingen. The avenue in which the attack occurred bears his name.)

Everywhere became aroused a resistance which was sooner or later to exhaust his power. He opposed Count Henri von Arnim, the new Ambassador from Germany to Paris, who, in his turn, as stubbornly opposed the views of the Chancellor. The conflict was terminated by the suppressing of the unfortunate von Arnim, who was condemned by the Supreme Court to six years' imprisonment, for having secured some diplomatic documents belonging in the archives.

In June, 1875, the Chancellor retired to Varzin, firmly resolved to disengage himself for a time from European politics. Indeed, the state of his health was such that it was only by strict obedience to the *régime* prescribed by Professor Schwenninger, the physician employed by him somewhat later, that the progress of the malady which threatened to undermine his health was effectually staid. (We shall have occasion again to speak of the physician who is to-day one of the medical celebrities of Germany.)

Exhausted by the continual warfare which he was obliged to maintain in order to insure the triumph of the anti-liberal theories of which he was the champion, fatigued, doubtless, by the weight of a career so contrary to his bucolic aspirations, he resigned from the chancellorship. The Emperor replied to the proffered resignation with a "Never!" which found an echo in many a German heart. But this word, it seems, was pronounced only for the gallery, so to speak. Privately, the matter was more simply treated; it even furnished Bismarck with a *mot* truly *piquant*.

The Emperor, remonstrating against the decision of his old servant, said:

"Eh! what? you pretend to be fatigued, overworked, too old—what not! Look at me! I am much older than you and I still ride horseback." "No doubt, Sire; that is natural;" replied Bismarck, "the rider always outlasts his mount."

In the year 1878 one of the events in the family-life of Bismarck was the marriage of his daughter, the Countess Marie, to Count Kuno von Rantzau; a marriage which, a year later, gave him the additional happiness of being for the first time a grandfather.

Upon the general condition of the family in 1881-82, we find some details in a letter written (December 27, 1881) by the Chancellor to the brother of his old *valet d'écurie*, Hildebrand; the same whose life the Lieutenant Bismarck had saved. Hildebrand had just died in America, and his brother, who also was there, wrote to apprise the Chancellor of the fact. The reply is worthy of being reproduced, denoting as it evidently does, in the man of iron, apart from a simplicity and natural ingenuousness which have already been noted, certain qualities of heart of which he appears to be little prodigal beyond the limits of the family circle.

My dear Hildebrand:
Your letter is received and I am happy to learn that you are well, although destiny has not spared you affliction. Your brother was older than I thought. In 1851 your wife was a quite young girl, she cannot then be very old; I am glad to know that you are living happily with her, and that she sometimes thinks of Germany. Augusta must have become a fine Yankee. With me all is going well, in so far that all my family, thank God, are living and in good health, and my daughter has presented me with grandchildren.

My sons, to my great regret, are not yet married, but they are well, thank God! I cannot at this moment say as much for my wife, still less for myself. I no longer hunt nor ride —finding both exercises too exhausting. If I do not soon decide to take some rest my vital forces will hold out but little longer.

What is your age? and how do you occupy yourself? supposing you have not retired from business. You may tell your wife that Lauenburg is prospering; I was there in the autumn for the first time in thirty years and was presented with the freedom of the city; upon the strength of which I send special greeting to your wife.

The two sons of the Chancellor in their turn shared the Imperial favour. Count Herbert was given a colonelcy, Count Wilhelm was made Commander of a squad. The former, besides, became under-Secretary of State at the Ministry of Foreign Affairs. The second, who embraced a governmental career, was granted a kind of prefecture. About the same time the Emperor solemnly conferred upon the soldier-statesman the military order *for merit;* the only German order which he did not possess, and which made the forty-eighth decoration which had been awarded to the Prince in the course of his career. From that moment it would seem as though Bismarck's popularity increased in proportion to the number of his enemies. To celebrate the seventieth anniversary of his birth (April 1, 1885), the Berliners organized a monster *fête*, truly national, which was to be repeated each successive year. The Government itself set the example. The Emperor, accompanied by the princes, presented himself at the palace in the Wilhelmstrasse, to offer his congratulations to his old servant and to embrace him; Bismarck afterward received the ministers, the deputies of his party and deputations from all the business associations in Berlin. Among the gifts and compliments which consecrated this unforgettable birthday *fête*, which even that of 1895 could not surpass, must be named as of greatest consequence the national subscription of 2,700,000 *marks*. With a portion of this sum the German people had repurchased the seigneurial domain of Schönhausen, of which the Bismarcks had been obliged to dispose during the hard times; the remainder, about a million *marks* in specie, was presented to the Chancellor to do with as he would.

The seigneurial domain of Schönhausen, the new one, so to speak, is about three times the extent of the original estate. The *château*, built in 1734, as indicated by the escutcheon surmounting the grand portal, is architecturally more elegant than the old one, and its arrangement is more comfortable. A rose garden extends along the principal front. On the day upon which the Chancellor re-entered into possession, he paused upon the threshold and said: " Here I often played with Hedwig *à la vie à la mort*, an amusing game in which whoever was killed continued none the less joyously to play his part."

With the disdain for comfort which characterizes him, Bismarck has never occupied his new possession—to-day transformed into a museum. During the rare and brief visits which he has since paid to Schönhausen, he has always stopped at the old patrimonial *château*. It is upon the little terrace bordered with century-old lindens, which extends along the front of the older mansion, that he has placed the five French cannon with which William I. presented him after the war of 1870-71.

These five cannon are: the *Navarin*, from the arsenal

The Terrace at Schönhausen, with the French Cannon taken in 1870.

at Douai, 1745, taken at La Fère; the *Ravissant*, from the arsenal at Douai, 1713, taken at Soissons. The carriages belonging to these two pieces are ornamented with a heraldic sun with scattered rays, and the device: " *Pluribus nec impar* "; the *Autorité*, a campaign piece, founded at Douai in 1856, ornamented with an " N " and the Imperial crown, from Metz; the *Champion*, a campaign piece from

Bismarck and his Son Herbert.

the arsenal at Strasbourg, 1862, taken from the suburbs of Paris; and a *mitrailleuse*, the *Général Malus*, from the arsenal at Douai, 1866, also ornamented with the Imperial cipher, and taken after the capitulation of Sedan. As to the individual gifts received by the Chancellor upon this triumphant occasion, it is impossible to enumerate them. A brewer sent the Prince a cask of Bavarian beer, the cask weighing two hundred and fifty kilos and containing one hundred and fifty liters of beer. A Herr Edenhofer von Regen—an original, he!—sent him an enormous organ-pipe, attuned to *la*, with an address, saying that the Chancellor had never had need of a diapason by which to accord the violins of the European concert but should this diapason ever be lacking the sender would be happy to know that his instrument had been of service. Organs, it seems, are the instruments best appreciated by musical Germans. Bismarck himself, so little master of arts in general, has, it is said, a weakness for—barrel-organs. He even one day presented one to the eldest son of the present Emperor. Going to visit at the Palace, upon the day following his arrival he observed that the little Prince had not acquired the " knack " of turning the handle.

" I will give you a lesson," said he; and shouldering the organ he ground out an air with amazing gusto, while the little Princes began to dance.

Prince William arriving upon the scene, regarded it astonished; then smiling at Bismarck he said: " Perfect! these little Emperors of the future are already dancing to your music! "

The anniversary of 1885 brought more serious gifts.

From Constantinople arrived a Turkish sabre incrusted with precious stones; an historic arm which had belonged to Ali, Pasha of Janina; upon the blade is the Arabic inscription: " Happy he who perishes by this sword: death by so perfect a blade will seem sweet to him." Bismarck laughed at this device and declared that according to his notions a long life was preferable to the most artistic death

Bismarck.

by violence; he should therefore endeavour to preserve both his life and the arm which might deprive him of it.

A number of inhabitants of the Harz Mountains sent him an enormous pipe of most delicate workmanship, accompanied by a quatrain in which the desire was expressed that the Chancellor would smoke in it tobacco cultivated in the German colonies. This pipe has long been the Prince's favorite, but it is doubtful if he has invariably observed the wish of its donors. Finally Tyras, the celebrated *Reichshund*, received for his personal use and decoration divers lots of collars and blankets—even a canopy.

This first of April was marked by another happy event, a purely family affair—the announcement of Count Wilhelm's betrothal to his cousin Sybil von Arnim, the daughter of that Malvina to whom her brother, Otto von Bismarck, addressed so many tender and witty letters. The marriage was celebrated on July 6th of the same year at Kroechlendorf; the Countess Wilhelm von Bismarck is now the mother of three children.

The years 1885 and 1887 were marked by some sensational speeches delivered at the *Reichstag*, where the Chancellor rarely appeared except when it became necessary to speak in defence of the military budget or to insure the consolidation of troops for the national defence. His furloughs were passed at Friedrichsruh, Kissingen and Varzin, where he occupied himself in rebuilding his paper-factory, which had been destroyed by incendiarism.

Then came 1888—a year of mourning and affliction; the sad prelude to his fall being the death, at an interval of three months, of the first two German emperors—the old William and his successor Frederic. On the day of the death of William I., the *Reichstag*, immediately assembled, witnessed the spectacle of Bismarck sobbing on the platform. The Iron Chancellor wept the death of his august master, but perhaps also—prophet that he was, accustomed to read the future, to interpret the mysterious signs of fate—wept he for himself and his **work**.

XI.

Court Holy Water—Bismarck Offered the Diploma of a Doctor of Theology—The Gods Abandon Him—His Farewell to Fontainebleau—The "Good Friends" are Turn-Coats—A Good Impulse of the Emperor—The Bottle of Steinberger—Triumphant Return to Berlin, and Platonic Reconciliation—The Patriarch of Friedrichsruh—Death of Mme. von Bismarck—The 80th Anniversary—A New Edition of the National *Fête* of 1885—The Sabre of the "Fear of God" Allegorizing the Sword of Damocles—Popular Gifts and Homage.

The accession of William II. to the Imperial throne did not at first appear to affect the *modus vivendi* of the Iron Chancellor. The young Emperor announced to the entire world his firm determination to worthily succeed his grandfather. He even seized the occasion of December 31st to send the " dear Prince " the warmest assurances of his friendship, asking all the blessings of heaven upon him and hoping, he said, that for yet many years they might work together for the grandeur and prosperity of the country.

But the diplomatic Bismarck even then divined, under all this rhetoric, the presence of a man who was to fight him upon his own ground, with his own arms; an Emperor who proposed to govern by himself, and who at least cherished the secret ambition of being *his own chancellor*.

Just here may be mentioned a fact which borrows from its date (November 10, 1888) a character of providential irony. Upon that date, which marks the anniversary of Luther, the Chancellor was awarded the diploma of Doctor of Theology by the University of Giessen. In the way of consolation for the approaching crisis, which was to send the man of the *Kultur-Kampf* back to private life, it was perhaps a trifle inadequate.

Bismarck after his Dismissal.

Another irony of Destiny shows us Bismarck, for the first time in his life, deceived in his habitual calculations and proclaiming his confidence in his star at the very moment of its setting; at the instant when the propitious gods were about to abandon him.

In October, 1889, at the conclusion of an interview which Bismarck had had with the Emperor Alexander III. of Russia, the latter said to him: " I should like to believe you and I have perfect confidence in you; but are you sure that you will retain your post?"

"Certainly, yes," replied Bismarck; "I am absolutely sure; I shall remain minister until my death."

Five months later Bismarck abdicated.

I designedly employ the word "abdicated," because the retirement of the Chancellor was of the character and importance of an abdication. The pretext alleged by William II. was lack of accord between his Chancellor and himself concerning the interpretation of certain articles in the Constitution of 1852.

On March 20, 1890, Bismarck was obliged to send in his resignation to the Emperor, although on the first of January of the same year the Emperor had despatched to the Prince assurances of his unalterable gratitude, accompanied by the expression of fervent hopes of their continued excellent understanding and collaboration.

The same protestations are repeated, indeed, in the letter in which his resignation was accepted, and which, while depriving him of all his functions, at the same time made Bismarck Duke of Lauenburg and Lieutenant-General of Cavalry, with the rank of Field-Marshal.

On March 26th Bismarck said farewell to the Emperor and to the Imperial family. The Berliners profited by this occasion to give him an indescribably enthusiastic ovation. His landau was besieged and bombarded with flowers, and the tumult at one moment became so excessive that, the horses threatening to bolt, Bismarck was obliged to descend

After a Family Dinner.

from his carriage to the bridge which led to the Imperial Palace.

Some days later he had an interview with his successor, General von Caprivi; an interview in the course of which the Prince is said to have said, in French, to the new Chancellor: "*La Roi me reverra.*" This prediction, in its threatening sense, has not been realized, and it should be added that Bismarck afterward denied its authenticity in the *Hamburger Nachrichten.*

The Prince did not wish to leave the capital without taking leave for the last time of the tomb of the old Emperor. He went to Charlottenburg, and, descending into the crypt of the mausoleum, laid some flowers upon the coffin of the man whom he had made a glorious and powerful Emperor. This pious pilgrimage was made on March 28th. On the same day Bismarck took formal leave of Count von Moltke. The final departure took place so precipitately that the German journals declared that the Chancellor had not been given the time necessary to effect his removal in proper form; hence the loss of numbers of objects of value; in short, his departure might be compared "to that of a German family expelled from Paris in 1871." An enormous crowd accompanied the landau to the station, where again burst forth the most marked manifestations of enthusiasm, which continued until the departure of the train for Friedrichsruh. Count Herbert, who, since 1885, had worked with his father in the capacity of under-Secretary of State, resigned his post in order to accompany his father into retirement, thus cutting short a most brilliant career, for he had been appointed Minister to Prussia in May, 1888, and seemed to be a most fitting person to one day succeed to the Imperial Chancellorship. Count Wilhelm retained his post of President of the Council at Hanover.

And, now that the curtain may be drawn upon the political

career of Bismarck, it is with a kind of relief that we see approaching the end of our task. The conclusion will be less painful to us because unaccompanied by those souvenirs, irritating to us, which attach to the political history of the Chancellor; it will be confined to the recording of the sayings and doings of his private life, which is itself irreproachable. Among the most characteristic words spoken by the Chancellor, à propos of his retirement, we quote the following: " All the ' good friends ' begin to breathe again and to sigh: ' At last! ' I am not to be pardoned for remaining Prime Minister for twenty-eight years! Twenty-eight years! —think of it! What insolence! [sic]. Should not such effrontery have been long ago discouraged? and all who, in those twenty-eight years have vainly hoped to become Prime Minister; all who have considered themselves ill-treated, misunderstood, unappreciated, or ill-recompensed—all approve; and God knows what total their numbers have reached in this long time!"

This enormous cohort of natural enemies, which the continued success of a man necessarily gathers in his wake, was as a matter of course employed in aggravating the misunderstanding between Bismarck and his sovereign.

So far was it successful that two years later, at the time of the marriage, in Vienna, of Count Herbert and the Princess Hoyos, the difference took a more serious form. The Emperor declared himself entirely uninterested in the event, and Chancellor von Caprivi sent a despatch to Prince von Reuss, Ambassador to Vienna, requesting him and his *suite* to abstain from all participation in the *fêtes* announced. This measure decided the Emperor of Austria himself, who was upon the best terms with Bismarck, not to be present at the marriage, which was celebrated with the strictest privacy. Despite his advanced age Prince Bismarck and his wife travelled to Vienna, and it is important to note that both going and returning the ex-Chancellor was greeted with enthusiastic warmth. The family passed the remainder of the summer at Varzin, where Bismarck received the sad intelligence of the death of his old friend and associate Lothar Bucher.

"All my friends," said he, upon this occasion—"my true friends—have preceded me to the tomb, and those who pretend to be my friends turn from me."

It was absolutely true, for it was upon the support of the one-time partisans of the Prince that the Emperor William II. continued to count, while his official enemies persisted in their opposition to the Government. It was evidently a tardy consciousness of this false position which decided the young Emperor to effect a reconciliation.

This was accomplished by the somewhat eccentric means of a bottle of old Rhine wine (Steinberger *Kabinet*) which the Emperor sent the Prince by his *aide de camp*, the young Count von Moltke. The ex-Chancellor was just recovering from an attack of pneumonia, contracted during a sojourn at Kissingen in 1893, and which, while he was slowly convalescing, was complicated, in January, 1894, by influenza and a return of the facial neuralgia from which he had formerly suffered.

Hardly was his recovery assured when Bismarck started for Berlin to offer his thanks personally to the Emperor who, in fact, had explicitly solicited an interview. This was for the Berliners the occasion of fresh manifestations still more enthusiastic than those which had preceded it. The people cheered both the sovereign and his old minister; and more than one partisan of Bismarck, witnessing this triumphant return to grace, must have been tempted to prognosticate the ex-Chancellor's return to power.

But it was decreed that all marks of the high consideration in which the supreme master of Germany was henceforth to hold the founder of the Empire should be purely honorary in character. Besides, was not Bismarck grown too old to dream of resuming the reins of a government which he had directed with such marvellous address? Undoubtedly, for he had nearly reached his eightieth year, and the most gifted imagination would have had difficulty in recognizing in the gentleman-farmer the martial colonel who spurred the King's horse at Koenigsgraetz. The caricaturists themselves would have had some trouble in identifying him, for he had long since lost the three hairs with which the top of his cranium had bristled. He was then a handsome, dignified old man, wearing, generally, the habit of a Protestant priest—a long, black coat, a neckcloth of white lawn and a broad-brimmed hat. His countenance, however, retained its expression of intense energy, and from his eyes occasionally flashed the same spark which had made so many human beings tremble. The old lion was not dead and could still roar were it necessary. No, he was not dead, but Death was about to pass so near him that the rustle of his wings would be heard, and to strike the devoted companion of his life, the stainless wife who for half a century had so simply and valiantly shared the burden of his success, the laurels of his glory. On November 27, 1894, Madame von Bismarck died of the malady which had for some months been undermining her health, and the old man of the Sachsenwald was left alone in the twilight of his life, deprived of that Johanna who had been as a beacon to his stormy existence; of the woman so tenderly loved, and of whom he had so often repeated that without her he would never have become what he had been.

His sorrow found an echo in the German heart; once more was it proved that it beat in unison with his own. The national *fête* which celebrated the eightieth anniversary of the old Chancellor's birth surpassed in brilliancy all which had preceded it. The Emperor himself set the example. Accompanied by the Crown Prince, he presented himself at Friedrichsruh, wearing the cuirass and uniform of the White Cuirassiers, the helmet surmounted by the golden eagle with outspread wings. Bismarck had donned for the occasion his cuirassier's uniform of the *landwehr*, and in the forest-bordered field where the encounter took place, the old soldier-statesman and the Emperor who looked like the hero of a Wagnerian legend, once more gave the enthusiastic crowd the illusion of assisting at an interview between two sovereigns about to seal the peace of the world. Faithfulness to historical fact makes necessary the remark that the Emperor's step had also for its motive the giving of a lesson and a warning to the leaders of the Parliamentary Opposition. As a matter of fact, some days before, the Government party, represented by the President of the *Reichstag*, Herr von Levetzow, had proposed to Parliament that the felicitations of the Assembly should collectively be offered to Bismarck. The Liberals and the Catholic party protested, and the Deputy from Hodenberg had mounted the platform and made the following declaration:

In the name of my political friends of Hanover, I pray the President to expressly except us, in addressing felicitations to Herr von Bismarck. It would not be proper for us to participate in the rendering of honour to a man who, violating the rights of the German princes and people, has made Hanover a province of Prussia.

The *Reichstag* putting this proposition to vote, it was defeated by 163 voices against 146.

The Emperor's reply was promptly despatched; on the same day he telegraphed the Prince:

To Prince von Bismarck, Duke of Lauenburg, Friedrichsruh:
I desire to express to Your Highness my profound indignation at the decision just taken in the *Reichstag*. That

decision is in direct opposition to the sentiments of all the German princes and people.   WILLIAM.

However, the indignant attitude of the Emperor was not so successful as he had expected it would be; the Liberals resisted this sting of the lash. One of the most important

The Princess von Bismarck (the Year of her Death).

Progressist associations of South Germany (that of Pforzheim, Grand Duchy of Baden) responded with a vote frankly hostile to the sovereign, saying:

"The Assembly expresses its profound regret that a con-

Under the Trees at Schönhausen.

stitutionally irresponsible person should have permitted the expression of an opinion opposed to the vote of the *Reichstag;* it also expresses the hope that before, as after, the *Reichstag* may make its decisions without concern as to whether they shall be pleasing or displeasing."

But neither the murmur of the wind of the Fronde nor the very literal rain which fell at Friedrichsrüh on the day of the Emperor's interview with the Prince (March 27th) succeeded in dampening the general enthusiasm. It was an unforgettable spectacle to the crowd which pressed round the field occupied by the cuirassiers of the guard, elbowed at every moment by a flying squadron of photographers, reporters and police, when the Emperor caracoled before the troops to the sound of trumpet and drum, drew his horse in beside the landau in which sat the Prince, and presented to him the sword of honour which was the Emperor's personal gift.

This sword, which many high personages have since admired at Friedrichsruh, is a golden cuirassier's sabre, upon the guard of which is the escutcheon of Bismarck, and upon the head of the hilt a miniature of the Emperor. Upon one side of the blade is engraved the Imperial escutcheon and this inscription: "To Prince von Bismarck, Duke of Lauenburg, upon his eightieth birthday." Upon the other side, in Gothic characters, is the famous phrase in the discourse of 1888: *Wir Deutschen fürchten Gott, aber sonst nichts in der Welt*—("We Germans, we fear God, but nothing else in the world").

Device of which this time the circumstance emphasized the arrogance, and by which the new sword of Damocles seemed to menace all who showed any disposition to trouble the peaceful digestions of the German people.

And while the Emperor complimented the Prince in a few energetic words, which doubtless contained allusions relative to the national industry of Prussia, the little Crown Prince, also in uniform, stood near the landau, a living allegory of the future of this soldier-race, for whom it would seem there is no salvation except in military enterprises. During the days which followed there was a repetition of the "*huldigungen*" of 1885; a colossal stream of delegates from all corners of the world to greet the patriarch of Friedrichsruh and deposit their offerings at his feet.

Among these offerings, besides the commemorative monuments in chocolate and nougat, and the patriotic "*motifs*" in confectionery, was a helmet manufactured from the skin of "the fretful porcupine" with all its quills preserved; a discreet allusion, it may be, to the ancestral device of Bismarck: "Let the herb flourish by the wayside and have a care of it, wayfarer, for it has thorns"; a butcher's "degree" conferred by the corporation of meat and pork butchers of Berlin; some buffaloes, the gift of the German colony in Cincinnati; a gigantic sculptured group representing a stag brought to bay by the leader of the pack, gift of the patriots of Anhalt; a collection of the reports of studies, conduct and application obtained by Bismarck when a student at the school of the Gray Cloister, the gift of the director of the pupils of that institution.

XII.
BISMARCK AT HOME.

At Friedrichsruh—The Old Man of the Sachsenwald—Bismarck, Peasant—Professor Schwenninger: How He Became Bismarck's Physician—The *Régime* of Salt Herring—The Patriarch's House —His Private Apartment—Painful Digestion—A Souvenir of the Past—Bismarck Speculating at the Bourse—Diplomatic Superchery.

Some years since, the tourist who might have chanced to lose himself in the Sachsenwald—the Saxon forest—might also have chanced to encounter a gigantic old man, amply booted and arrayed in a long black coat or a gray plaid; chest expanded and walking-stick passed horizontally behind his back and through his bended arms. At once the tourist would have recognized Bismarck; the Bismarck millions of times pictured in this accoutrement of a pastoral hermit—a sylvan patriarch. Moreover, the presence of Tyras or of one of his compeers would have dispelled any lingering doubt of Bismarck's identity.

Nowadays, the old man of the Sachsenwald, a victim of rheumatism, seldom goes out; further, he has materially altered, in the physical man, from the likeness with which the world is familiar, and has more the appearance of a simple old peasant.

Bismarck no longer disdains the appellation of peasant, the highest honours having exhausted for him all their seductions. Did not the venerable von Moltke add that title (of peasant) to his signature? Bismarck would assuredly do the same did not he find it simpler to sign himself only " von

Bismarck," he who has an *embarras de choix* among the titles belonging to him. He is a proud example to the nobility of all nations.

The hermit of Sachsenwald, besides, has always retained his taste for simplicity and rusticity; caring as little for excessive decorations, because he may claim any number of them, as the man of many titles cares for those enviable distinctions. His attire is of the most modest description; he wears not even a ring.

Formerly, when he was able to take long walks and ride much, Bismarck's pride was in his well-varnished boots; now, even that bit of coquetry is denied him, for the old man passes three-quarters of his time in slippers, his legs extended upon a leather-covered footstool.

Now is the moment to speak of Bismarck's physician, the famous Professor Schwenninger who is the unanimously accepted medical authority in Germany. Yet it was not always so. His rapid rise, above all his nomination as Professor of the Faculty of Berlin, made him greatly envied, it is said even brought him enemies. Curiously enough, the grievance which medical men laid most stress upon was his Jewish extraction, which, as a matter of fact, he cannot claim. He owes his Semitic profile to his Italian origin. Early rivals, however, have yielded before the increasing popularity of Professor Schwenninger, particularly since an Imperial decree accorded him an unlimited furlough before permitting him to consecrate himself entirely to the service of Bismarck. It is considered that this physician has saved the Chancellor's life, a fact which has in no small degree contributed to disarm the prejudice of his colleagues.

Professor Schwenninger has founded at Berlin an Institute which has many students. His decisions are respected as if they were a sentence pronounced by the Faculty, and his advice is followed as implicitly as though he were an oracle. He has also a numerous *clientèle* which he treats by correspondence, for he seldom leaves Friedrichsruh. Communication with the Hermitage, moreover, is as assured as in the days when Bismarck was Chancellor. Most of the German post-offices close at eight or nine o'clock, while that of Friedrichsruh remains open until midnight or, on the great Bismarckian *fête*-days, does not close at all.

Bismarck at Kissingen.

It is enough to say that the voluminous daily mail of Professor Schwenninger is never delayed either in its receipt or delivery. Prince Bismarck enjoys truly princely privileges; a telegram sent by him to any station along the line of the Hamburg and Berlin railway will cause the most rapid express, which stops at no intermediate station, to be held at Friedrichsruh, that tiny village of at most a hundred souls, not to be found upon any geographical chart. It is unnecessary to say that Bismarck exercises his omnipotence only when he expects guests on the train. But this detail will suffice to give an idea of the respect with which the illustrious old man is surrounded in his retirement. Let us return to Dr. Schwenninger in order to relate an anecdote of the beginning of his connection with Bismarck. The reputation of the Professor was in its infancy when he was

Bismarck at Kissingen Station.

called for the first time to the Prince's palace, to attend his son, Count Wilhelm. Schwenninger cured the Count and was finally consulted by Bismarck on his own account; but the first serious consultation brought about an incident which was nearly disastrous. Schwenninger began by asking the Prince so many questions that, finally losing patience, he exclaimed: " Are you going to question me much longer? I asked to be relieved of my malady and not to submit to an interrogatory." The young physician, however, was not to be intimidated. " If I question your Excellency it is that I may be aided in discovering upon what ground to base my treatment. Yet if your Excellency dislike to be questioned you are at liberty to employ a veterinary, who is accustomed to cure his patients without ever asking a question."

The Prince shot at the daring young man a terrible glance, yet submitted, nevertheless; contenting himself with the retort: "Very well, so be it; do as you will. I have only one wish, and that is that my cure may result, and so prove to me that your talent equals your insolence."

Schwenninger had the unhoped-for luck to cure his patient.

The word "luck" is here not improperly used, for in these matters chance plays a more important *rôle* than may be supposed. It should be observed, however, for the sake of fairness, that the Prince's health was seriously compromised before he determined to mention his condition to the young physician. He was visibly wasting away and the physicians first consulted had pronounced the trouble a predisposition to cancer of the stomach and liver; in short, the Faculty had given the family to understand that the sick man had but a short time to live.

The first effect of Dr. Schwenninger's intervention was to raise the spirits of his patient and to reassure the family.

After his diagnostic the cancerous theory was disposed of, there having been revealed only a considerable dilatation of the stomach and intestines. Now Schweninger, who is an enthusiastic upholder of rational therapeutics, that is, of that which recommends hygienic and dietetic remedies before all others—was precisely the man for the situation; the "right man in the right place" as the English say. The treatment ordered was most rigorous. It consisted exclusively of an almost absolute dietetic *régime*, which was conscientiously followed by the sick man, who became docile the moment he was spared the swallowing of the drugs of which he had a horror. For six consecutive weeks Bismarck consented to live only upon salted herring, to which were afterward added butter, bread and potatoes. Fluids were interdicted until, his returning strength permitting him a little exercise, the doctor thought he might be permitted, one hour after eating, a few swallows of spring water.

This course was wholly successful, for the patient was not long in recovering and was enabled to resume his usual mode of existence. These details show that Dr. Schwenninger really saved the Prince's life and that the gratitude since felt and expressed by the Bismarck family is founded upon a solid basis.

Friedrichsruh is now to be described—the most modest of Bismarck's domains—of which he once thought to make but a simple country-seat, afterward deciding to pass there the remainder of his days. The motive of this decision has never been explained, and by nothing does it seem to be justified; neither the doubtful beauty of the location, which admits of a view neither extended nor picturesque, despite the Sachsenwald; nor the mansion itself, which to the minimum of comfort adds every imaginable inconvenience, including the small rooms which, built almost upon a level with the ground, even the monumental chimneys fail to render entirely free from humidity; added to these drawbacks is the immediate proximity of one of the noisiest railways in Germany; so near is it that the noise and smoke of all the express trains of the Berlin-Hamburg line enter the master's bedroom, at the extreme end of the house, only about thirty paces from the railway. The Prince is not wholly indifferent to these inconveniences but it is well known that he possesses a remarkable power of passivity to oppose to the contingencies of material existence.

He still occupies himself with tree-planting—the saplings in the near-by nurseries, awaiting the day when the centenarians shall have succumbed to the axe and they shall take possession of the vacant places, are sufficient proof. He insists that persons of his age do not build; he prefers to leave that duty to his sons. In reality, I believe in Bismarck's attachment to Friedrichsruh is to be found the simple fancy of an infirm old man who, having spent the greater part of his life in journeying, resists the idea of further displacement; finally taking root in the spot most propitious to his health. For him as for many others, doubtless the maximum of well-being is represented by a minimum of suffering; and this minimum supposedly corresponds with the meridian wherein lies the Duchy of Lauenburg.

There is no comedy in his obstinacy. Bismarck might as easily cultivate his garden at Varzin, at Schönhausen or in any other of his Thebaïdes, each more æsthetic and more conveniently arranged than Friedrichsruh. If he lives at Friedrichsruh it is, as we have said, simply an old man's caprice, strengthened by hygienic prejudices more or less illusory; it is also because he there feels himself much nearer Berlin, the heart of Germany—Berlin, which possibly continues to exercise over the old diplomatist that nostalgic charm which Paris, from a distance, exercises over every true Parisian.

In the course of a journey across Germany I was granted from the sleeping-car a glimpse of Friedrichsruh, and that vision left the same impression since found to coincide with many descriptions from the pens of German reporters. The edifice belongs to no known architectural epoch; it has nothing in common with the most rustic or modest *château*, and I can sympathize with Bismarck's vexation at being called by a certain celebrated writer among his compatriots —"the *châtelain* of Friedrichsruh"; in fact, said by any except an admirer, the title might be considered an ill-natured jest.

If one turns toward the wall of the park which extends to

the edge of the railway, the Prince's mansion is presented from its most favorable side. Here one of the wings constructed over an old court-yard, offers a sort of belvedere from which Bismarck can easily address the innumerable deputations which come thither to offer their homage. These deputations are almost never admitted to the house itself, access to which is rigorously interdicted to the profane, and generally to all visitors whoever they may be—with the exception of officers in uniform; Bismarck never having been able to cure himself of his partiality for a uniform.

If the threshold of the home is so carefully guarded, it is, let us say, uniquely to protect him from a repetition of the indiscretion of one anonymous admirer, who, as a souvenir of his pilgrimage, appropriated the manuscript which contained the good-wishes of William I. upon the occasion of Bismarck's sixtieth birthday.

Directly upon the belvedere opens the door leading from the dining-room, which also communicates with the large *salon*. Thanks to the numerous tall windows overlooking the park, the dining-room is very bright and cheerful in spite of the gray paper which covers the walls of this and every other room. The generally severe tone of the interior, particularly in the apartment occupied by the Prince, the mediocrity of the decorations and the slight degree of comfort, harmonize with the note struck by the exterior. In other respects, also, is confirmed that poverty of sensuousness and of artistic taste of which Bismarck has frequently boasted, alleging that the qualities which make an artist are incompatible with those which distinguish a statesman.

Upon the walls of the dining-room are paintings, chiefly landscapes, by Menzel and by Lenbach. Bismarck also counted upon placing there, in pursuance of the desire of the donor, the portrait of William II. sent to him by the

Emperor in 1890; but the canvas was too large. It is now in the museum at Schönhausen, together with the numerous other gifts received by Bismarck in recent years.

The windows of the *salon* entered from the dining-room also open upon the park; here it is that the family and guests gather after meals. A large divan occupies one corner of the room, which was formerly the favorite seat of the master of the house. Every evening he dispensed there the wit and gayety which accompany good digestion, surrounded by a circle of intimates of whom he was the venerated god—an illusion completed, moreover, by the clouds of smoke exhaled from his lips and from the bowl of his pipe, and in which, at moments, he totally disappeared.

Nowadays the digestion of the patriarch is more difficult and less complete; his humour less sociable and equable; failings for which now and then he asks to be excused, praying those about him not to take too much to heart his nervousness and his peevishness; "it is the effect of age and of the evils which it induces—but with me it never lasts long," he says. And the better to earn his pardon, no doubt, he willingly retires after dinner to a little room alongside, where he reads the journals until overcome by drowsiness.

The old soldier-diplomatist has truly an ancestral regard for his younger guests, for their gayety, in which he fears to strike a false note, for their pleasures which he would not embarrass. In the evening, indeed, the members of the family with their friends make up a little party at cards, and the presence of the old man would be a restraint, for Bismarck has never liked cards since he was very young;. in fact he disdains all games. Once only, according to his own avowal, he essayed some speculations at the Bourse—before he became Minister; but he had so little success that the experiment was never repeated.

It was at the time when Bismarck was charged with a mission to Napoleon III. *à propos* of the Neufchâtel affair. Being upon the point of declaring war against Switzerland, the Prussians endeavoured to obtain permission for their troops to cross the eastern provinces of France. Bismarck, convinced that the war would take place, gave Rothschild

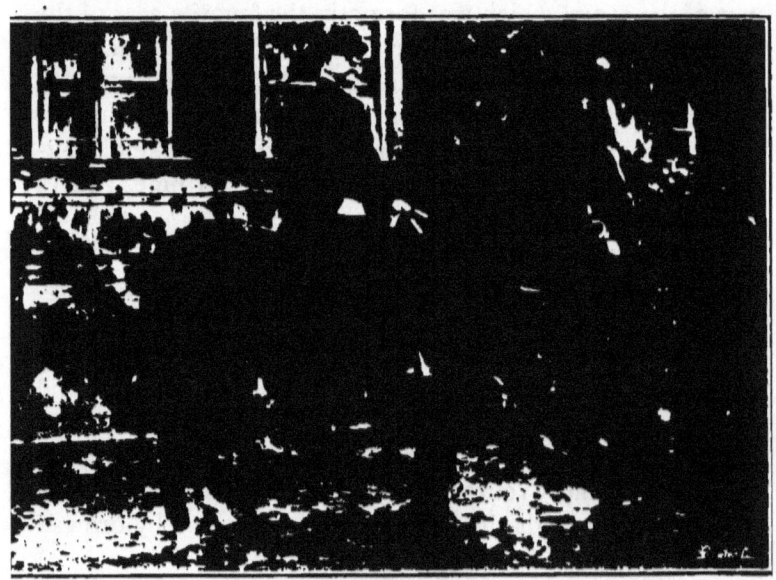

Starting for a Canter.

of Frankfort orders to sell. Rothschild disapproved of the proceeding, but Bismarck would listen to nothing and persisted in the order. The war did not take place, there was a rise in stocks and the imprudent speculator lost a large sum.

À propos of cards, the Prince once related to Herr Busch an incident worthy of Machiavelli, and to which his imagination doubtless added. It was at Gastein, in 1865, during the negotiations of the Austro-Prussian Convention.

The Last Interview.

Between times, parties were made up for the evening. One evening I myself made one of the fifteen, playing with a kind of folly intended to impress the gallery. This folly was entirely feigned; Blome, the Austrian diplomat, had pretended the day before that gambling furnished precious psychological indications of the moral value of the players. I resigned myself to the loss of a few hundred *thalers* expressly in order to give him an indifferent opinion of me. He thought he had to deal with an imbecile and a foolhardy fellow and this permitted me to get the better of him in the negotiations which followed.

Speaking of games of chance, Bismarck assured Herr Busch that he liked them when he was younger, but only when the stakes were high; "*It is a taste unsuited to a man who is the father of a family.*"

Let us mention, in passing, another room near the *salon*, where are arranged some objects of art and gifts peculiarly dear to the Prince; notably a smaller reproduction, in silver, of the national monument of Niederwald, a gift of the Emperor William I., accompanied by the words: "The keystone of your politics, souvenir of a ceremony especially in your honour, at which you were unhappily unable to be present."

Among the pictures is a portrait by Lenbach of Bismarck as the hermit of the forest, wearing the familiar gray visored cap.

XIII.

Bismarck's Bed-Chamber—Tyras I., Tyras II., and Rebecca—The Dogs' Paradise —Bismarck as a Zoöphile—Weighing and Measuring Machines—The Variations of the Chancellor's Weight—The Bismarck Family are Measured—Bismarck His Own Barber—The Sitting-Room of the Late Princess—Nocturnal Pastimes—Laborious Annexations—A Village Without a Barber, a Pastor, a Mayor, a Church or a School—Bismarck, Manufacturer of Wooden Paving-Blocks—Sylvan Legends: the *Horla* of the Saxon Forest.

The private apartment of the Prince, containing only strictly necessary objects, is situated upon the first floor in a distant wing of the building; his bedroom and study occupy the corner nearest the railway; a sort of antechamber leads to these two rooms, which serves as both reception-room and library; there are, however, few books there besides political pamphlets and works upon agriculture. Upon the walls are portraits of Thiers, von Moltke and the young Emperor William II., in the uniform of the red hussars.

The appointments and decorations of the study are not less severe. An enormous desk stands in the middle of the room, with ink, paper—all the necessary furnishings, even to the traditional goose-quill. Bismarck has always insisted that to use steel pens cramps his fingers. Not far from the desk stands a little card-table—the same upon which were signed the preliminaries of the peace of Versailles, and which the Prince bought of Mme. Jessé. Upon this table or upon the desk is not rarely seen a bottle of fine champagne, the Prince having become habituated to combat by this means the effects of the dampness or of excessive cold. Cognac is, as we have said, the Prince's favorite beverage.

The walls are covered with family portraits and those of Frederic the Great, William I. in civilian's attire, William II., etc. The only articles of furniture are a divan and an armchair.

The bedroom is the most characteristic of Bismarck himself. The venturesome person who could discover the means of evading the vigilance of Pinnow, the valet, and succeed, in the master's absence, in crossing the threshold of this modest wing, might penetrate without further difficulty into the sanctuary in question, for a thick carpet deadens the sound of footsteps, as in all the other rooms. Yet he should not prematurely felicitate himself upon his success for the bed is usually guarded by Tyras or by his spouse Rebecca, and the visitor would not meet an encouraging reception.

The present Rebecca is the descendant of the Rebecca mentioned in one of the letters already quoted. Her father, Tyras I., was the authentic *Reichsund*, which has nothing in common with the present Tyras. This fellow is a gift of the Emperor William II.; were it not for that fact Bismarck would long ago have disposed of him, for the dog is supremely displeasing to him.

"Tyras," he says, "is ungracious; his lips are too thick and he constantly froths at the mouth. I should never have bought such a beast."

Herr von Bötticher, who executed the commission, must be an indifferent *connoisseur*. As to Rebecca, she is of truly fine breed although already becoming too fat.

It must not be supposed, however, that Bismarck expresses his opinion of the Imperial gift by ill-treating poor Tyras II. He loves animals too well to do that, and is the first to acknowledge the good qualities which counterbalance his bad ones; for he is peculiarly gentle, his disposition is cheerful and equable and he is friendly with everyone, even those he sees for the first time. The single fact of finding the two dogs lying on the divan or in the master's chair is sufficient proof of his fondness for them.

Even at Berlin Tyras I. was present at all the informal receptions, although the animal was not always in a happy frame of mind and occasionally showed his teeth to an intruder who, to his mind, had not been duly presented. The master could never bring himself to punish the dog for these unsociable demonstrations; contenting himself with saying to the persons against whom they were directed: " This animal will end by setting me at odds with everyone!"

The violent passion of Bismarck for his dogs must be borne in mind, for—as I believe I have elsewhere said—it is a characteristic to be found in most humorists. Upon a little console is the portrait of a black greyhound; the famous " Sultan " which for many years was the statesman's intimate companion and mute confidant (the dumbness of animals is undoubtedly the strongest appeal to the sympathy they awaken in us). Sultan having one day attacked a passing chimney-sweep, was killed outright by the latter. His agony so unnerved Bismarck that Count Herbert thought it best to try to induce his father to leave the dog; but the Prince, meeting the tearful supplication in the poor brute's eyes—that terrible, poignant regard of dying animals—remained beside him, saying to his son: " No, I cannot quit him like that! " When Sultan had breathed his last the Prince, wiping his eyes, murmured as if to himself: " Our ancestors' religion was generous; they firmly believed that in the hunting grounds of Paradise they should find all the good dogs who had been the faithful companions of their life. I wish I could believe that."

With a less narrow conception of nature the hermit of the

Sachsenwald should have been able to add this one more to his Protestant beliefs; for it is confessedly illogical to believe that a future life is reserved for man alone, to the exclusion of all the other creatures of God.

Bismarck is not only a lover of dogs, but of birds, large and small, except birds of prey, which rouse the instincts of the sportsman. All others he protects, observing their habits with the interest and solicitude of a naturalist. All the crows, magpies and *sansonnets* in consequence adore the

The Museum at Schönhausen.

shades of Friedrichsruh, where they nest and go about their affairs in absolute security.

Upon entering the Prince's bedroom two articles of furniture attract the attention; a weighing-machine and a kind of dynamometer. The weighing-machine serves to weigh the Prince daily, in pursuance of his physician's orders; the use of the other instrument is easily divined; it resembles an enormous barometrical cage which reaches nearly from floor to ceiling. By pulling upon the handles suspended at the end of cords a weight is lifted a certain

Bismarck with his Beard.

number of feet. It is excellent exercise, requiring serious effort and admirably developing the muscles of the chest and upper extremities.

The weighing-machine which registers the variations in

the Prince's weight has always played an important *rôle* in his physiological experiments: for it should not be forgotten that Bismarck once weighed two hundred and forty-seven pounds and that his sojourns at Kissingen had for their chief purpose the reduction of this obesity. His perseverance was finally rewarded, for after a long time maintaining points between the extreme limit (two hundred and forty-seven pounds and two hundred) his actual weight sank even below that minimum. Berliners even demonstrated their interest so far as to erect a tablet bearing the record of these annual variations in Bismarck's weight; an incident which goes to prove the fanaticism of the Germans for their great man—their "*unser Enzige*" as they say.

The obsessions which in nervous temperaments leads to the formation of certain habits, the daily repetition of certain acts, led Bismarck to include his entire family in his own system of weighing and measuring. The measuring-machine, of which we have still to speak, is permanently fastened to the wall of another room. The Prince one day amused himself, December 31, 1880, by having all his family pass under this instrument, with the results given below:

Bismarck	1 metre	880
Count Herbert	1 "	860
Count Wilhelm	1 "	851
Count Rantzau	1 "	780
Mme. von Bismarck	1 "	714
Countess Rantzau	1 "	716

As this demonstration proves, the average height of the family is very respectable; few families in France could exceed it. Bismarck's stature is exceptional even in Prussia, which explains the surprise of Prince William in 1847, when the young Referendary was first presented to him.

The hereditary Prince could not refrain from saying: "It appears that the civil government is at present recruiting its referendaries from the royal guard"—which was composed of the tallest men in the country.

The furniture of the bedroom, which is very simple, includes the bed—a rather large one; a wardrobe, a monumental dressing-bureau, a divan and an armchair exclusively for the use of the dogs; some wooden chairs, a cheval-mirror and a set of shelves laden with brochures and "bedside books"; among the last the German writer from whom these details are borrowed, affirms that he has seen a Prayer-Book and a volume of the "Meditations" of Luther; even a kind of religious almanac in which are inscribed the Prince's own daily meditations. If this be true one may be permitted to attribute these practices rather to a praiseworthy desire upon Bismarck's part to render himself worthy of his degree of Doctor of Theology than to a genuine devotion, which must have been somewhat tardily inspired.

A door near these shelves leads to the Prince's wardrobe-room and to Pinnow's chamber. The word wardrobe-room here employed is distinctly hyperbolical, for the room contains little besides rows of boots and some old coats.

Before the mirror which has been mentioned the Prince used every morning to attempt to shave himself; for until late years he has always shaved himself; now his hand is doubtless too unsteady to perform so delicate an operation, and upon the valet probably devolves that duty; I say "probably," because it is a mere supposition. A supposition, however, which is likely to prove true when it is remembered that there is no barber at Friedrichsruh and that the male population of the village is reduced to availing itself of the weekly services of a journeyman barber. Bismarck has worn a beard but twice, once when, at Kissingen, rheumatism disabled his right arm; and afterward at Varzin, during

The Master of Friedrichsruh Visits his Domains.

an attack of facial neuralgia; but his face was then made so unfamiliar by the sudden appearance of a white beard that he has never since consented to wear one.

The same misadventure arrived, it is said, to the Emperor William II., who, in the course of a trip North, permitted his august cheeks to be invaded by a pair of side-whiskers such as his illustrious grandfather wore; but as they rendered him unrecognizable he was forced to have them instantly removed for fear of further compromising his Imperial dignity.

The family portraits so numerous in other rooms are more scattered here; noticeable, nevertheless, is one of Mme. Bismarck; another of Count Wilhelm as a youth; an engraving of the poet Uhland and finally a magisterial portrait of Dr. Schwenninger, by Lenbach.

Other pictures represent still-life or studies of animals; their presence is satisfactorily explained by the naturalistic tendencies of the master. The last room, more or less connected with the Prince's apartment, is the *boudoir* of the late Princess; yet the word "*boudoir*," employed by the German writers, does not describe such a room as would call for the use of the word by us; for we are told that in this "*boudoir*" took place the interminable conferences of the Princess with her *chef*. At present it contains a desk and chair, from the back of which depends a funeral crown sent by the Emperor of Germany. The desk, which has nothing in common with the furniture appropriate to a boudoir, was the Princess's work-table where she kept her household accounts in order, recording in various little blank-books her numerous small economies, which censorious German tongues pronounced avarice.

The room has not been changed since the death of the Princess. Beside the desk stands a marble statue of the Prince. The pedestal is now covered with innumerable photographs of illustrious persons and many crowned heads, all accompanied by autographs—the collection overflowing upon a neighbouring table.

To return to the Prince's bed-chamber, it is actually so near the railway that the passing of an express shakes its walls. Perhaps the old man likes to hear its thunder rolling through his sleepless hours, and is grateful to it for dispersing the phantoms and for overcoming the heavy silence of certain nights, now that he has no longer the resource of hard work, as was formerly his wont. He once made the following admission to a friend:

"The silence after midnight is terrible; it arouses all the wicked spirits within me and makes me a victim of my own fancy; to escape them I am obliged to rise and read or write. Often, at such times, have I imagined in advance the whole course of a discussion, first permitting my adversaries to speak, then replying with arguments so pertinent, so unanswerable, that, fearing to forget them I have risen and made a note of them; yet never, never have I been able to make use of those arguments; they were too subtle to be appreciated by the generality of practical men; no, the paper and ink beside my bed were uselessly wasted. Not until the first sounds which accompany the break of day are heard do I fall asleep."

From this it may be supposed that Bismarck is not an early riser; nevertheless he is up by ten o'clock and at once has his mail opened while he completes his toilet or eats his first breakfast of eggs, tea or coffee. The employment of his day, which formerly consisted in long walks and rides, is now confined to an occasional outing, for the old man suffers greatly from rheumatism.

We must now speak of the little village of some ninety or a hundred souls, disdained by geographers yet represented nevertheless upon the wall of the *Landhaus* by an official placard so prodigal of topographical and administrative information that its like for expansiveness is vainly sought along the great roads leading to our most considerable *sous-préfectures*. I give herewith an exact copy:

> ### FRIEDRICHSRUH
> *Gutsbezirk Schwarzenbek*
> *Amtsbezirk Friedrichsruh*
> *Kreis-Herzogth: Lauenburg*
> *Reg-Bez. Schleswig*
>
> | Landwehrbezirk | Lubeck |
> | Hauptmeldeamt | Caserne. |

This, as will be seen, furnishes all the indications relative to the state—civil, administrative and military of the commune, and may serve as model for the reforming of our departmental and parochial sign-boards.

At Friedrichsruh, however, it may be considered a superfluity, the few houses of which the village is composed, with the exception of the railway-station, being exclusively the property of Bismarck and inhabited without an exception by his own *employés*.

These houses, it is said, Bismarck has acquired by a long and persevering system of annexation.

When the present Duke of Lauenburg—the Duchy itself originated from a contestable annexation, because it was a part of the price of the victory of the Prussian army over the Danes—took possession of his domain, he applied to his subjects the system of optional expropriation; that is, he purchased all the houses which their proprietors would consent to sell for money. Two small ones only refused his advances and, although the master was well-versed in such matters he was obliged to wait, the demand appearing to him excessive.

Did the recalcitrant subjects recognize that it was to their benefit to permit their properties to be annexed by the

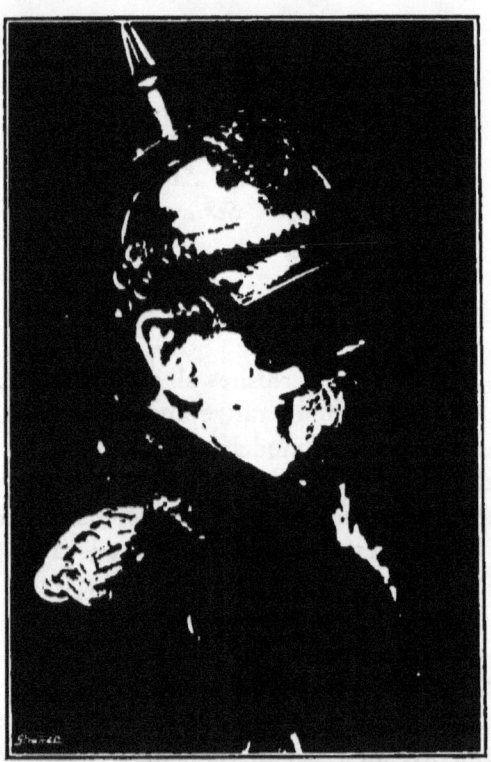

Bismarck as Colonel of the Landwehr.

Prince? apparently not, for they resisted until 1885, it is said, in which year a number of Hamburg notables purchased those properties for the sum of 40,000 *marks* and offered them to the Prince upon the anniversary of his seventieth birthday.

The Salon of Friedrichsruh, April 1, 1893.

Now, therefore, the entire annexation of the village is an accomplished fact; the inhabitants of Friedrichsruh are all the Prince's subjects, forming in this out-of-the-way corner of the earth a kind of feudal phalanstery, the members of opposite sex marrying among themselves and taking root in the place. In this there is a certain advantage, for it is not easy to be married at Friedrichsruh. Not only is there no barber, but there is neither church nor pastor. In order to obtain the benediction of the Church, the contracting parties are obliged to make a little wedding journey " before the letter " of twenty minutes in the *Bummelzug* [omnibus], to Schwarzenbek. Formerly the sacraments were administered by the chief-forester, which made the ceremony a civil function; now Count Rantzau, as Mayor of the commune, performs that service.

It is a singular commune, indeed, for there is also an absence of schools, and the " natives " are forced to send their progeny to Auenmühl, half-a-league distant, if it is desired to give them even the most meager instruction. On the other hand, the roads and paths through the forest swarm with foresters in uniform and busy wood-cutters, whose business it is to fill the great steam saw-mill two steps from the railway-station.

This very important saw-mill, founded and managed by the Prince himself, turns out annually a million of *marks'* worth of wood, the greater part of which is destined for the paving of the large cities. In Rome and Berlin are some streets so paved; not, it is said, to the unqualified satisfaction of the Berliners.

The mill in question, notwithstanding its profitableness, gave the Prince some trouble in the days of his chancellorship, and it frequently happened that the smaller industry hampered the success of the great national industry of which the diplomatist was then the chief purveyor. The reporters of that time represent the Prime Minister as interrupting his interminable conferences with the head-forester in order to settle with all haste the affairs of Russia, Austria and France, or to regulate his accounts with England; then

Bismarck in 1894.

plunging again with enthusiasm into a study of the most practicable ways and means to convert into paving-blocks the centenarian timber of the Sachsenwald. Nowadays the older trees are more respected. The aged confraternity seconding, Bismarck is more willing to spare old trees, old people and old animals. The Sachsenwald, in which are to be found all varieties of trees—oaks, elms, pines, chestnuts, birches, beeches—the full-grown ones extending over a total area of eight thousand *hectares* [over sixteen thousand acres] is divided into several lots, the larger number of which is preserved for hunting or converted into parks for the raising of game. The forest itself is agreeably diversified with hills rising here and there, and cleared spaces from which a glimpse is had of a sparkling lake idylically framed in its sylvan surroundings; with tiny vales where the forest is more dense and where beneath the tall trees which form a continuous arch, wind clear brooks filled with excellent trout.

Doubtless the greater number of legends of good and evil genii—gnomes, sylphs, dwarfs, ghosts, etc., who, according to tradition, inhabit the forest, is a direct legacy from the Middle Ages; yet there are also modern ones. Such is the fantastic "*Waul*," a kind of mysterious *Horlà* who goes about with two dogs. Old inhabitants are said to have seen one of these dogs forgotten and left by him under a bed; it was a hunting dog, spotted black-and-white. He remained for a year stretched out in the same place, never touching food, only growling when a man or other animal attempted to approach him. Then he disappeared as he had come, carried off by the *Waul* in one of his nightly rounds. There is also a white horse which wanders freely in the forest, his head reaching above the tallest tree; his appearance is generally the herald of misfortune. Neither Bismarck nor his family has encountered it.

XIV.

At Varzin—Under the Trees—The Château and Park of Varzin—Bismarck's Sense of Precision—Mistaken Vocation—Falls from His Horse—Cerebral Pathology—Too Much Postal Matter—Bismarck Imitates Mr. Herbert Spencer—The Village Inn—The Mysterious Staircase—How Bismarck Evades Importunate Visitors—Personal Pride—The Opinion of a Belgian Diplomatist—Lugubrious Avowals.

"Forests all resemble one another"—has said a celebrated thinker: "their appearance gives one the same illusion as that supplied by human life itself. From afar, they have an imposing air; they are full of mystery and seduction; when one penetrates them it is to find one's self simply among trees." This relieves us of the duty of describing the forest of Varzin, which, with an added note of picturesqueness, in every way resembles the Sachsenwald. There are to be found the same arches of verdure, the same jungles of tall beeches and pines, the same rushing streams, the same pools—with, indeed, one more—a marshy lake, covered with reeds and water-lilies, which extends along the foot of the wooded hills connecting the villages of Varzin and Wussow.

The Prince's *château*—for Varzin is a genuine castle although not particularly imposing—is situated a little beyond the village, from which it is separated by the park and the high-road. It consists of an old seigneurial mansion to which a more modern construction was added after 1871, provided with two wings, their walls finished in yellow rough-cast. A large terrace, ornamented with a double row

The Chancellor's Dogs.

of dwarf palms, leads to a court of honour and to the verandah where the Prince generally receives his visitors. This verandah itself communicates with a conservatory which opens upon a garden of curiously designed beds.

The park extends beyond the garden with its wooded terraces, its extensive greensward sloping gently upward, ornamented with statuary and crowned with a small, airy temple, from which there is a beautiful view. It includes more than forty acres planted in oaks and beeches, and reaches to a little river which, half-a-league farther on, feeds the mills already mentioned. Access is gained to the park by a little bridge thrown across a lake stocked with gold-fish, trout and carp.

The interior of the *château* reveals at the first glance its superiority to Friedrichsruh in point of comfort; even the decoration of the rooms displays a more artistic taste. In the Prince's study all the furniture is of old oak and Renaissance in design. The walls are wainscoted with oak to the height of two metres. A monumental fireplace in green *faïence* occupies one of the corners. It was constructed especially large that whole tree-trunks might be burned in it. Upon either side of the chimney is a collection of escutcheons which also serves to ornament; among others, that of Alsace-Lorraine, and the modern escutcheon of the Prince with the famous motto chosen by himself: "*In trinitate robur;*"—and another, Protestant, form of "With the aid of God, by the grace of God," which is incessantly repeated, like the *leitmotiv* in music, in the letters and informal conversation of Bismarck.

A divan extends along the wall opposite the door. A long table placed before this seat is covered with brochures and numerous maps. Bismarck has always had a passion for topographical and ethnographical maps. The same instinct of mathematical precision which induces him to constantly consult thermometers and barometers to learn in what temperature and under what atmospheric pressure he is living, which induces him to attach considerable importance to the figures which represent to a millimetre his exact weight and height, makes him unable to support the idea of following a path, the *détours* of which he does not know in advance; or of venturing into a country of which he has not previously studied the physical aspect and the ways of communication. Never has he or any member of his family started upon a journey without having first studied the maps, and he invariably selects the shortest and most comfortable route.

The walls of the study are adorned with souvenirs of the war of 1866—paintings and photographs. The desk stands near one of the windows which opens upon the court of honour. A shell [obus] serves as a paper-weight; there is also a tobacco chest, bearing, carved in relief, the head of the famous "Sultan" whose tragic death was related in an earlier chapter. It should be observed that the details here given belong to the period when Varzin was the country-seat habitually occupied by Bismarck; some of the objects mentioned have since been transported to Friedrichsruh. Even the study has been abandoned to Count Herbert's use and occasionally serves as a reception-room.

Among other rooms is to be mentioned a brilliantly-lighted dining-room, a most artistically gilded *salon* and a billiard-room. The halls and staircases connecting the two rooms are decorated with the antlers of stags, deer, mouflons —trophies of the chase which are the personal souvenirs of the Bismarck of other days.

When the Chancellor spent his summers at Varzin he led a life which would exhaust the most active temperament. His vacations brought but an increase of work of which our Excellencies who retire to their country-seats for rest can have no idea. He spent his mornings interviewing alternately his head-forester, the gardener, the architect, his familiar councillor Busch and the superintendent of his three mills, Fuchsmühle, Hammermühle and Campmühle. The forester particularly then became the *âme damné* of the Chancellor, whose passion for sylvan beauties is already known, which has led him sometimes to say: "I should have been a forester, I have missed my vocation." Hunting and long rides were then naturally the favorite distractions of the *châtelain* of Varzin. An accomplished horseman, Bismarck rode a furious pace the instant he was in the saddle. It was the *tolle Yunker* [mad squire] of earlier times which then reappeared in the diplomat. A dangerous delight, however, were these mad gallops; they resulted in more than fifty falls, some of which were terrible. The last occurred near Varzin when the Chancellor had three ribs broken.

"As to falls," he once said to Mr. Busch and his colleagues, "I had one which was followed by extraordinary results, proving how far human thought depends upon the physical state of the mind. We were returning from the chase one evening, my brother and I, pushing our horses to the utmost; suddenly my brother heard behind him a great noise; it was my head coming in contact with the road.

"My horse, startled by a carriage backing toward him, had shied, reared and fallen over backward. I lost consciousness and when I regained it I was in a state of waking somnambulism. A part of my faculties remained unawakened. I examined my horse; the girth was broken; I mounted the horse of the whipper-in and we returned to the house. The dogs greeted us as usual with joyous barks. I did not recognize them, and mistaking them for strange animals threatened them with my whip.

"I then related that the whipper-in had fallen from his

horse and gave the order to go and seek him with a litter; as I was not obeyed I became furious and reproached my brother for his inhumanity; I felt at the moment as though I were both the whipper-in and myself. Dinner was served, and I sat down with a good appetite; then I went to bed and sleep restored me, for the next day I remembered nothing about it."

The case is not so extraordinary as Bismarck thought. These phenomena—of partial amnesia complicated by a doubling of the personality—frequently follow traumatic accidents and the recent works upon the pathological physiology of the brain throw sufficient light upon them.

The two manufactories, of which pictures have been given, are situated at the distance of half-a-league from Varzin upon the little river Wipper. The water-wheels supply the force utilized in the mills to convert the wood cut by the foresters into paper and *carton-pâte*. This paper, unlike the paving-blocks made at Friedrichsruh, is greatly liked in Germany, and orders at certain seasons arrive in such numbers that the mills are insufficient to fill them all. The products of these paper-factories have enabled Bismarck to reduce the considerable expense attendant upon the acquisition of the estate, its aggrandizement and repair.

After the reports and consultations of the morning came the visits to the plantations, fisheries and farms which furnished all the provisions, except wine, consumed at Varzin. This picture of the Prince's energy would, however, be incomplete if mention of the occupations which he created for himself were omitted from those more elegant, created by his numerous correspondents and visitors.

What figures will suffice to give an idea of the various calamities attached to the popularity which so many enemies have envied Bismarck. In a single year the appeals for charity addressed to him amounted to nearly 2,500,000 dollars, and the post-office in the village transmitted to him 650,000 letters and 10,000 telegrams.

This record is enough to discourage the most robust man. Finding it impossible to make headway against such an overwhelming postal delivery, even by retaining his secretaries and himself working late into the night, he resolved to

The Last of the Chancellor's Rides.

insert prohibitory notices in the journals, which, however, discouraged none.

More recently, Mr. Herbert Spencer, in England, has been obliged to have recourse to a similar expedient; he has addressed to his correspondents (and perhaps continues to address them) printed circulars, informing them that his ill-health and a lack of time obliges him to decline replying to all letters concerning his personality, his occupations, his ideas or his works.

As to visitors, Bismarck had no other resource against them than to rigorously close his doors against them, as he still does at Friedrichsruh.

This was the origin of the vogue which the little inn in the village enjoyed, for it served thereafter as a refuge for the visitors who frequently prolonged their stay three or four days in the hope of forcing an entrance at an unguarded moment. After the attempt of Kullmann a guard was placed permanently in the inn, following the Prince from place to place. This arrangement, however, did not prevent the visits of the more persistent pilgrims from being renewed again and again; among them, it is said, were sometimes illustrious persons whose names and personalities were protected by an incognito; there were even women, who left upon the imaginations of the good people of Varzin an impression of romantic mystery.

When Bismarck was surprised by a visitor who, by one means or another had succeeded in effecting an entrance, he disappeared by a subterranean staircase probably leading to the cellar. One day when Herr Busch arrived at the *château*, he saw the Prince engulfed in this passage and asked him if he were descending into the *oubliettes*.

"This staircase," said Bismarck, "serves me as a means of escape from the unexpected bores. Hearing your postilion's horn I was preparing to eclipse myself, forgetting that you were to come to-day. You have no idea of the life these importunate people lead me. A fellow sent me word one day that if I refused to receive him he would go out and hang himself. I was exasperated and replied that if that painful extremity appeared to him inevitable I would have a fine, strong, new rope sent him, but that he should not see

The Old Man of the Sachsenwald.

me. And the man, be it understood, did not hang himself." The Prince had still another method of evicting persevering visitors which has given rise to a very amusing anecdote, whether or not it is true.

A foreign ambassador had been for a long time in conference with the Chancellor when it occurred to him, during a pause in the conversation, to ask Bismarck by what means he rid himself of pertinacious callers. "Oh, it is very simple," replied Bismarck; "when my wife thinks the audience too long she sends for me upon some urgent pretext and the individual is obliged to raise the siege."

As he finished speaking a domestic entered and begged his master to accord the Princess a few moments. The ambassador very nearly lost countenance and perhaps even Bismarck himself was a trifle disconcerted by the irony of the coincidence; at any rate the interview was promptly terminated by the departure of the foreign diplomat.

And now would the reader know Bismarck's opinion of his own activity?

The following characteristic detail, reported by a guest at Varzin or at Friedrichsruh, it matters not which—will tell us. One day while at table a telegram from Berlin was handed to the Prince, who rose directly, begging his guests to excuse him as the telegram required an immediate reply. "For you see," he said, "this telegram is from my son Herbert, and if I do not reply he will send me a second and a third; he will not leave me an instant in peace until I have answered. Herbert is pitiless; he knows only duty and will not admit that one may be freed from its laws. If I had, in my youth, been as active as my *filius* I should have been still other than I am."

In spite of all these qualities Bismarck was very severely judged by his colleagues in diplomacy. The following citation is what the late Baron von Northumb—then ambassador from Belgium to Berlin—wrote of him in 1877, when the Oriental question reappeared upon the horizon of international political preoccupations:

As to the *rôle* which Bismarck will play in this question, all that is to be said is that he is dominated by the fear of a Franco-Russian alliance. Had he an elevated mind and a generous spirit, one might be able to conjecture, but the Chancellor is not guided by the interests of humanity nor even by those of Europe. For him politics is but a dynamic force. He disdains mankind; he has but two objects: to accomplish his work; the grandeur of Germany and his own. He says he is profoundly unhappy, and he is. His equilibrium is destroyed. He has just made a pretence of wishing to renounce his power but he would not know how to live without it, without the admiration of the public, and he proves it by the attention which he pays to the press. The slightest attack irritates him. I search vainly for his counterpart in history. The man cannot be judged without taking into consideration his temperament as it has been developed by his unprecedented success. His power has become a kind of ministerial Cæsarism. He would have good health would he consent to apportion his time and his occupations more conformably with reason, and better understood self-government. He goes to bed at four in the morning, to sleep at seven, and rises in the afternoon. By that time business has accumulated and he regards the labour before him with repugnance, even with anger!

The picture may be a trifle dark, yet at the period during which Baron Northumb wrote these lines Bismarck himself had begun to doubt the wisdom of his work and was overcome at times by an indescribable melancholy. His biographer, Herr Busch, paints this state of his mind in moving lines, which we here transcribe without commentary:

"It was at Varzin, in 1877; the twilight was falling and, according to his custom after dinner, the Prince was seated near the fireplace in the large *salon*, where stands Rauch's statue: 'Victory distributing Crowns.' After a prolonged silence, during which he from time to time threw pine-cones on the fire, looking straight before him he began to lament that his political activity had brought him little satisfaction and still less, friends. None had given him credit for what he had accomplished; his work had brought happiness to

To Bismarck—Erected by the Students of Germany.

none; to himself, to his family, to none that could be named. Someone replied that he had at least made the happiness of a great nation. He sadly shook his head as he replied: 'Yes, but how many people have I made unhappy? were not it for me, three great wars would have been avoided, eighty thousand men would not have perished; fathers, mothers, brothers, sisters, widows, would not have been plunged into mourning. *It is a business between God and myself*, but I have reaped little or no joy from my exploits; nothing but vexation, disquietude, chagrin.' He continued in this tone some time longer, while his auditors were silent and surprised, never having heard him speak so; and while the 'victory' seemed to be throwing her crowns to the old man, we thought of the discouraged lamentations in Ecclesiastes; 'Then I looked on all the works that my hands had wrought, and on the labour that I had laboured to do: and behold, all was vanity and vexation of spirit and there was no profit under the sun.'

"The Chancellor has since frequently thus expressed himself," adds Herr Busch; "and almost in the same words."

XV.

ICONOGRAPHIC NOTES.

Mr. John Grand Carteret has published a very complete and attractive work upon Bismarck in caricature. There are to be found, ingeniously classified and commentated, most of the fancies by which designers the world over have been inspired through the *faits et gestes* of the giant of German politics.

My own task is infinitely more modest, for the simple reason that the caricaturists have rarely attacked his private life, as it has offered little temptation to that satirical fancy which is necessarily the note of all caricature. Tradesmen more than all have exploited the political Bismarck. The heads of Bismarck upon nutcrackers, inkstands, paper-weights, in Swiss wood carvings, are generally heads of a helmeted ogre in no sense representative of the handsome features of the old hermit of the Sachsenwald. The same may be said of the heads upon pipes, which represent the martial Bismarck; the severe effigy of the statesman-cuirassier.

True, the greater number of these objects belong to the period before Bismarck had retired from the direction of Germany; yet again in 1894 was to be found among the commercial advertisements of German journals, mention of a certain liquor called " German Unity," presented under the auspices of a patriotic design representing the eternal Colonel of Cuirassiers, arm in arm with the Emperor William II.

Our readers who know the weakness which Bismarck had

for this uniform will not doubt that he saw with pleasure the universal consecration, in graphic art, of his military type. Little did it concern him that it should appear in a grotesque, caricatured form. It enhanced his popularity and that sufficed.

The most generally caricatured man of the age, with Na-

Liquor Amenities of United Germany.

poleon III. and the Sultan, has never felt the slightest resentment against his caricaturists; perhaps in this indulgence is to be discovered the humorist's secret sympathy with all forms of humour.

A short time after the death of Napoleon III. the Sultan

intimated to European cabinets that the pertinacity of the caricaturists in taking him for a "Turk's head" was highly displeasing to him. Possibly he expressed himself in more diplomatic language, but these are almost the words used by Bismarck to translate for the benefit of his intimates the

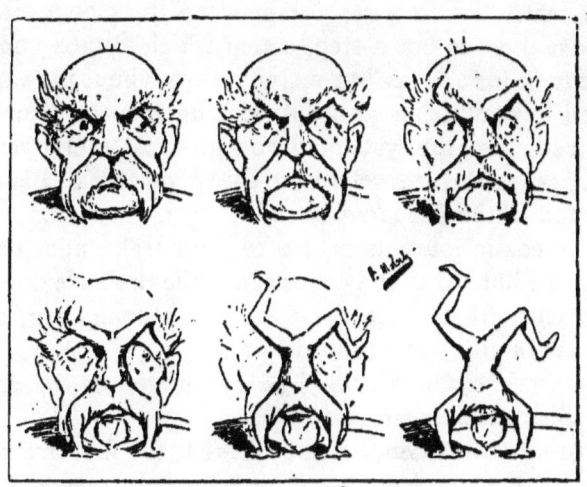

What is to be Seen in the Face of Prince von Bismarck.

ideas of the "Commander of the Faithful;" and he added: "Napoleon dead, the Sultan in hiding, I shall remain the only prey of those gentlemen." Then, fearing that he might be misunderstood, he continued: "Not that I am uneasy about it—on the contrary! I am merely wondering whether I shall suffice for them."

If we are to regard the psychological *leit motiv* developed in the preface to this book and which reappears in most of the chapters, according to the good Wagnerian formulum the first place here should be given to a caricature by Moloch, conceived after the Lavaterian process, which consists in discovering unexpected likenesses in salient features —progressively denaturalized—of the human face.

It is seen by our engraving, that in applying this process to Bismarck's face, the designer, Moloch, finally evolved from it an acrobatic figure poised upon his two hands, with his legs in air; an acrobat, a rope-dancer, a clown, if you will, consequently a humorist; for between the clown and the humorist there is but a step, a step which Prince von Bismarck took for a " yes " or a " no " throughout his career.

But I have anticipated in introducing this caricature, because it supports my system. I now go back several years.

The first caricatures relative to the private life of Bismarck are found in the *Kladderadatsch*, of 1872. Previous to that time the comic journals presented Bismarck under terrible forms, as a lion, or as the cat asleep while the mice dance, or as a blacksmith forging fire-arms; as a conqueror, a mechanician, a pilot, an equilibrist, etc.

The *Kladderadatsch* should be considered as the creator of the Bismarckian caricature.

A curious coincidence is the fact that the first great caricature of the *Kladderadatsch* in which Bismarck figures (1849) represents the future Iron Chancellor (at a period when he little dreamed of possessing that title) as a mailed crusader. But this redoubtable crusader, who holds in one hand his genealogical tree, in the other his rod, shows at the same time—a fine allusion to his retrogressive ideas—the suggestion of a crawfish in the antennæ which spring from his helmet and the cotyledonous tail falling over his heels. The entire caricature is a satire directed against the patrons of the *Gazette de la Croix*, founded by the feudal nobility as a reaction against the revolutionary movement of 1884 and to assist the triumph of absolutism and divine right.

Note this detail, which is of real importance to the history of Bismarckian caricature. Until 1862 Bismarck was pictured with a head of hair and a beard; but the hair rapidly diminished and was replaced, in the designs of the *Kladderadatsch* by the point of a helmet. On May 5, 1862, Bismarck, sent as ambassador to Paris, began to shave.

From the following year appeared the three legendary hairs, of which the *Kladderadatsch* is the creator. This journal claims the distinction in a poem addressed to Bismarck in 1880, *à propos* of a fine incurred by one of its artists

First Appearance of the Three Hairs.

for the " offences to the Chancellor." Here is the strophe in which appears the claim and which points the iconographic history of Bismarck:

" Qui t'a posé sur le front plus d'une guirlande de fleurs?
Qui a chanté plus d'une chanson en ton honneur?
Qui t'a paré de la triple aigrette capillaire?
Celui-là même que tu viens de prendre pour cible.
Ton courroux de deux javelots de crible.

Le premier transperça, ô tristesse amère,
L'auteur de tous tes portraits, homme irascible,
Le second heureusement se perdit dans le sable . . .
Non, Otto, de ta part ce n'était guère aimable."

In 1872 the same *Kladdcradatsch* exhibits the first rural Bismarck. Tyras sleeps with his head resting upon the knees of his master, who is crumbling some bread for the geese that are flapping their wings at his feet. The *châtelain* of

The Rustic Appears in Fine Weather.   The Soldier Appears in Storm.
A Barometrical Fancy.

Varzin at the same time holds over his head an umbrella to protect himself from the shower of letters and telegrams with which the air is filled.

In 1876 a barometric fancy shows us the Colonel of cuirassiers alternating with the good rustic in Calabrian hat, according as the weather is dry or wet. Then by little and little the pipe and the bock appear and finally is risked a caricature of the Bismarck of the Parliamentary receptions or as the forester of Friedrichsruh.

A new vignette by Daelen represents the postman entering the *château* of Varzin. The wagon is overflowing with

Bismarck is Proud to Discover upon the Head of his Eldest Son the First of the Three Hereditary Hairs.

its burden of bales, cases, packages, casks of beer, sent to Bismarck from all corners of the German Empire.

In 1884 the *Kladderadatsch* produced an engraving treated with immense seriousness in which for the first time Bismarck appeared as the father of a family. He is seeking in the head of his son Herbert the first of the three patrimonial hairs.

He has, it is said, especial theories concerning hair-cutting; theories based upon the influence of the moon at certain seasons, which the diplomatist has simply borrowed from the forester which sleeps in him.

Once when one of his councillors, Herr Abeken, had his hair cut, Bismarck felicitated him upon the improvement in his appearance, saying he had chosen a good time for the operation, that is, at the change of the moon.

"For you see," he said, "some hair is like trees. When the roots should survive the tree is felled in the first quarter; when they should decay it is cut down in the last. Some people, particularly savans, do not believe this, but the Department of Forestry observes the practice while it does not admit the principle."

Whether from deference, from habit, or from tradition (and caricature is necessarily observant of physiognomy, being forced to stereotype certain gestures, attitudes, salient features which afterward figure among the comic attributes of the personage) the artists continue to plant the three prophetic hairs upon Bismarck's cranium, where, in reality, they are no longer to be found. Here is even a design from the *Lustige Blätter* which represents them as piercing the rock where the new Barbarossa is hidden. The following lines explain the particular symbolical significance of the composition:

> Le nouveau Barberousse
> Qui s'est retiré, grondant,
> En son château de Friedrichsruh
> Se tient caché maintenant.
>
> Il a renoncé à trôner en maître
> Au sommet de la chancellerie;
> Il y retournera peut-être,
> Mais à sa fantaisie.
>
> En une chaise d'ivoire
> Lourdement assis,
> Le prince appuie son front de gloire
> Sur une table d'onyx.

The Real Bismarck.

Du fond de sa pipe austère
Il tire de vrais nuages.
Et les trois cheveux du sage
Ont percé la voûte de pierre.

The New Barbarossa.

Il dit au docteur: "Mets-toi
A cette lucarne pour inspecter le monde
Et dis-moi ce que ta vue profonde
Retient ou aperçoit.

" Et si le peuple des corbeaux, hélas!
Plane encore audessus de mes précipices,
Eh bien, j'attendrai, de guerre las,
Des temps plus propices."

The crows, Caprivi and Bötticher, are sufficiently recognizable; but the head of Dr. Schwenninger which appears at the small opening in the rock is the best of all.

A Paternal Lesson in Diplomacy.

But the date of his retirement is not yet reached; a date naturally signalized by a recrudescence of purely political caricature; free from malice, as it should be when applied to an old man supposedly upon the eve of complete disgrace.

The *Kladderadatsch* represents him for the last time in uniform, giving his son Herbert a lesson in diplomacy; and the scene, I do not know why, appears to be laid in a cave among a confusion of voluminous folios.

On the next page of the "Bismarck Album" are seen Richter and another leader of the Opposition beginning to take off his boots.

Other precursors of the approaching fall are revealed to us by the pencils of the *Kladderadatsch* artists. Here is a partial eclipse of a lunar Bismarck, announced by the telescopes of the principal German journals. The shaded face which overlaps a good third of the well-known round one, crowned with its three heraldic hairs, is that of Count von Waldersee, the Chancellor's great rival.

Another fancy of the same period, which was a remarkably perfect achievement quite above the plane of caricature, is Bismarck in rustic attire (the Bismarck of Lenbach's very life-like portrait) standing in the middle of a field filled with superb cabbage-heads. The scene is laid at Varzin, to which the Chancellor made a short excursion, and where, said the legend, he should be happy to be able once more to contemplate heads which were not those of opponents or dissenters of any kind.

Finally the hour of retreat sounded and the caricatures became philosophical. . Germany, which criticised him harshly enough some years later, described his abdication in the most *bourgeois* manner imaginable, with a humorous emotion quite ludicrous. The little dwarf of the *Kladderadatsch* wipes his eyes with one hand and holds out the other to Bismarck (in civilian's dress, valise in hand) who lays in it three hairs, for he has just relinquished all the insignia of his rank and desires to owe no man anything.

The French allegories which greeted his departure are more gloomy. A design by Willette shows the Chancellor in full uniform under a coat of mail, holding a halberd. The dog is seated behind him. Both are guarding a fantastic park full of cannon and shells and Bismarck launches these proud words at Death, who is passing: " In spite of the cold I am always the guardian of this flock. Death! go thy ways!"

A trifle less somber yet quite as bitter, is " The Four Seasons of a Statesman," by J. Blass. Republican France (for the female figure which symbolizes it wears the Phrygian cap) is playing with a jumping-jack with the features of Bismarck and his three hairs; she holds him by these hairs with

The Farewell of the *Kladderadatsch* (1890).

one hand and with the other pulls the cord which makes him dance. At the end of the first season the legs fall; then the arms and finally, by winter-time, nothing is left but the head; the jumping-jack is demolished. The allusion, to my mind, is not so clearly indicated.

The Italian journal, *Il Pasquino*, simply shows us the Chancellor preparing his troupe of marionettes for removal.

" Punch," in which the humour is always of a serious character, almost tragic when it refers to politics, published,

The Dismissed Pilot.

March 19, 1890, a very beautiful caricature of " The Pilot Dismissed," standing upon the ladder at the ship's side, while over the railing above the Emperor William leans and looks after him sadly. The "Judge" represents the Chancellor closing his shop, uneasily regarded by Gladstone; while "Moonshine" shows the same persons "turned out" in a pelting rain which they stoically face. Naturally Bismarck is a molossus and Gladstone a griffin; the anthropomorphous heads of two dogs have a gloomy expression of melancholy resignation and, one of them, of ferocity.

In the Swiss caricatures humour is the chief note. The Helvetian Bismarck appears generally on top of a mountain, occupied in contemplating the various countries, the sight of which starts afresh the wounds of the thwarted politician. (The *Nebelspalter*, of June 15, 1889.) At the last turn, he is carrying his favorite son Herbert and leading the other by the hand; but his strength forsakes him and the giant falls; he is finally borne to the grave upon four needle-guns. (The *Carillon* of Geneva.)

The other foreign caricatures are gay and amusing, and neutral as to politics.

Years have passed and the German caricaturists are becoming hardened against their great man. The *Lustige Blätter* in particular is aggressive in tone. In 1893 appeared a page containing eight coloured designs, comparing the Bismarck of an earlier day with the Bismarck of this later time. The words of the latter (for he is now satisfied only to talk) are the exact contradiction of his former acts; the whole constitutes a most successful satire upon the chameleon-like Bismarck with whom our readers are acquainted.

First comes the Cuirassier-Diplomatist of 1866, dropping into the great bag of Prussia all the little States ripe for annexation: Schleswig, Hanover, Frankfort, etc. Beside this is the hermit of Friedrichsruh, in dressing-gown and slippers, drinking with the delegates from Lippe to the long life of his grandchildren. Below is Bismarck as Jove the Thunderer, striking down all who resist him (particularly

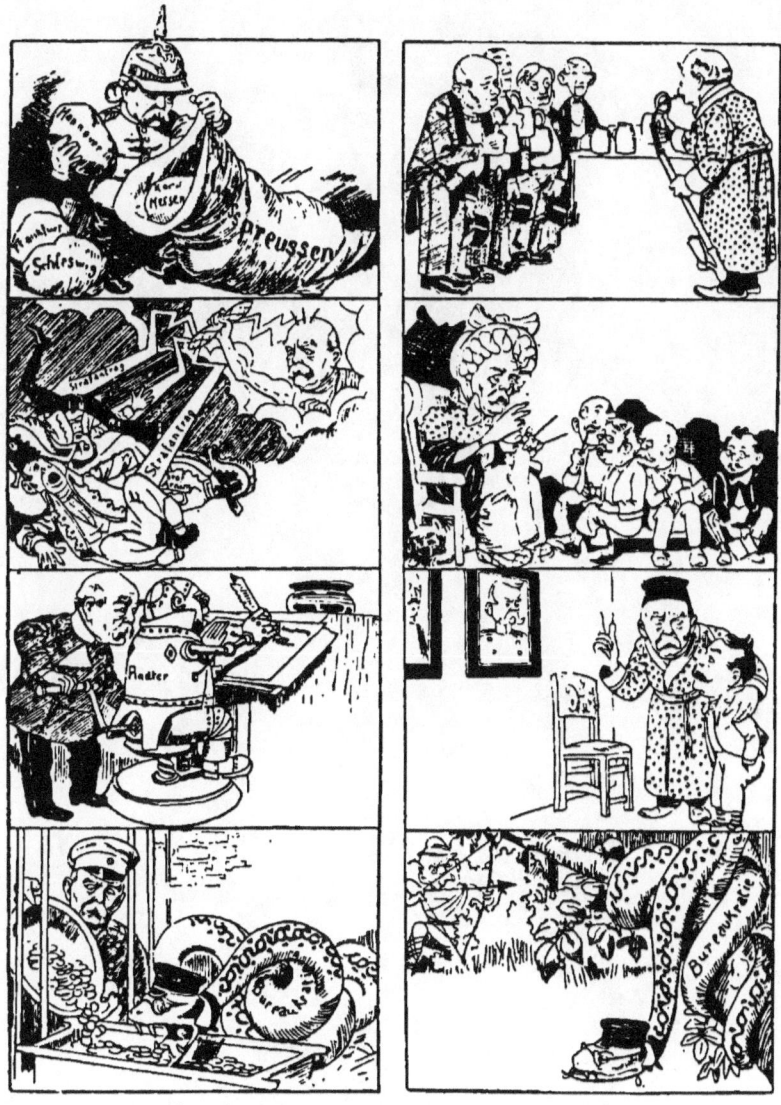

Formerly. To-day.

Evolution.

Count von Arnim); beside it is the same man, disguised as an old grandmother and relating to her guests this sentimental legend: " There was once a good old time which was called antiquity: in that day there was no danger in leading the Opposition." The third design presents Bismarck as the officious father of the press, turning the handle of the

The Prodigal Son.

automaton Pindter that he may eject one more " leader " ; next it, is the old man in a dressing-gown, showing his son Herbert the portrait of Caprivi and saying: " Look here, my little Herbert, if ever you become Chancellor, do not imitate this man, who retains his power only by suspicious practices,

208   The Real Bismarck.

and principally by influencing the press." Finally comes Bismarck the conqueror, filling with gold-pieces the boa-constrictor bureaucracy, while beside it, as a huntsman, he

Memories of Youth.

Début upon the Political Stage of Frankfort in 1851, in the Character of Mephistopheles.

pierces this same reptile hoping to strike in a mortal spot the frightful glutton.

The project for a commemorative monument to Bismarck,

presented by this journal in 1893, did not exhibit more respect for the idol of Germany. " Since he may not have an equestrian statue," says the article, " that style of monument being reserved exclusively for the members of the reigning family, and as a representation of the great man on foot would not be sufficiently imposing, we take the liberty of submitting to the benevolent attention of our contemporaries the accompanying designs."

First appears a coupé without a horse attached, in which Bismarck is seated facing his dog; the carriage has as a pedestal an enormous triumphal arch. Next is Bismarck upon a colossal bicycle: then Bismarck astride his dog Tyras; again he is mounted upon a headless wooden horse (like the gymnasium dummies); and at last the horse is inserted in spite of the restriction, only Bismarck remains standing beside the beast.

The satirical socialistic sheet, *Le Vrai Jacob*, is really less hard upon the great man; as the " Prodigal Son " it shows us a rustic Bismarck guarding a drove of pigs, each one of which bears the name of a journal still faithful to his cause.

In 1894 the tone of the *Lustige Blätter* softened. In a large coloured engraving we are presented to the ex-Chancellor draped in the *burnous* of Moses. The angel of the German nation is standing beside him, pointing out to him the new palace of the *Reichstag* and saying: " There is the Promised Land to which thou hast led thy people, but thou shalt not enter it."

The great reconciliation was about to take place, however, and the *Lustige Blätter* effectually altered its tone.

The grand event was epically treated, the two champions appearing in the costumes of Achilles and Agamemnon. Achilles speaks to Agamemnon in the language of Homer, assuring the latter that his wrath is appeased because an ir-

Bismarck has his Boots blacked by all Classes of Society.

A modern Gessler Desires to have his Helmet Saluted by All, but the New Tell, the *Reichstag*, Refuses.

reconcilable attitude is not appropriate to noble minds. He ends by grasping his antagonist's hand, amid the acclamations of the Roman people.

Other sketches, equally benevolent, illustrate the events of that memorable week ("*Bismarck's Woche*"). The caricaturist of the *Lustige Blätter* invented apocryphal extracts from illustrated journals. From *L'Ottomane* he cut an illustration of Bismarck as a charlatan, accompanied by this idolatrous inscription: " The Prince appeared, in this time of sickness, like the physician of the miracle; the entire world received him with acclamation, sure that he was the bearer of the panacea capable of curing all the ills of the universe."

From the hypothetical *Mécontent*, a socialistic sheet, is Bismarck the Imperial architect, out of a job; he is ringing at Caprivi's door to ask if the Premier is likely soon to have vacant such a trifle as a chancellor's post. Another clipping, supposedly from the journal *Le Vaisseau de l'État*, shows Bismarck and Caprivi together turning the wheel which guides the rudder, and it is predicted that a fusion of the old and the new era is about to be accomplished.

The caricaturist of the *Lustige Blätter* copied once more, purporting to be taken from " The Vine," which represents Caprivi weeping into a bottle of " Steinberger, Kabinet " which the Emperor is about to send Bismarck, the inscription explaining that the famous bottle thus contained Lacryma-Caprivi of 1894.

From that moment the acerbity of the German caricatures was converted into dithyrambics, and the allegories inspired by the great *fête* of 1895 (the eightieth anniversary of Bismarck's birth) were exclusively laudatory and hyperbolical.

The *Lustige Blätter*, once so cutting, presents the Imperial Chancellor in three successive guises: Bismarck, a giant among dwarfs; Caprivi, to whose height the dwarfs of yesterday have attained; and the Prince von Hohenlohe, a dwarf among giants, who are no other than the dwarfs of yesterday.

This idea, in another form, appeared in the same sheet in 1897. It represents Bismarck the giant that he was as, at the same time, Prime Minister and President of the Council. "To-day," reads the legend, "every effort is being made to fill this colossal mould, but without success."

Great Success in 1870-71, in the *Rôle* of Siegfried.

The design shows Chancellor Caprivi and the President of the Council, Bismarck's two successors, vainly attempting to stretch themselves to the height and breadth of their predecessor.

Upon the occasion of the anniversary *fête* of 1895, the enthusiasm of the German caricaturists attained its height.

The satirical socialistic sheets alone held out, yet even *Le Vrai Jacob* contented itself with picturing the idol of Germany receiving the homage of all the monopolists.

The *Lustige Blätter* led with a special number, containing a large engraving covering two pages and representing

Bismarck, Tailor and Bootmaker.

Bismarck's apotheosis. The Iron Chancellor is on horseback, preceded by two heralds-at-arms, one bearing an escutcheon with the device: "*In trinitate robur,*" and the other a shield upon which is inscribed the famous apothegm: "We Germans fear God," etc.

The first page of the same number is consecrated to a correct and extraordinarily insipid sketch which proves at least that German caricaturists gain nothing by departing from their methods. Bismarck holds Germania in his arms, who, kneeling upon one knee, is offering him a sumptuous crown of flowering laurel; conspicuous in the foreground is the Chancellor's gigantic pipe, the only humorous detail of the composition.

Here, then, is the situation between Germany and Bismarck clearly defined—from the caricaturist's view-point.

The *Fliegende Blätter* followed in the footsteps of its *confrère* with another and less-clear attempt at a Bismarck apotheosized.

Le Rire of the same date gave a masterly page vibrating with patriotism, by Jeanniot; and in the following number reproductions from the *Kladderadatsch* and other journals displaying Austro-Hungarian pictures. The latter, as may be supposed, were less tender of Bismarck. The inscriptions accompanying the designs which we have copied render a further analysis of them unnecessary.

XVI.

BISMARCK BEFORE POSTERITY.

The melancholy avowal which, in 1877, escaped from Bismarck's lips, should not surprise the reader now familiar with the various states of conscience of the man whose more intimate life has just been sketched in bold outline. Under the inscription by von Moltke in an album:
"*Le mensonge passe; la verité demeure*" [Lies die; truth lives] —Prince Bismarck traced this ironical reflection:
"I know well that truth will be victorious in the other world, but in the meantime a field-marshal himself would be powerless against the lies in this world."
It would be impossible to more wittily praise the arms in use, although Bismarck has often declared that he gloried in the ability to say that he had never lied. As a matter of fact the words "truth" and "lie" are equivalents in politics, and signify one thing or quite another according to the country. For this reason we may doubt the sincerity of Bismarck's pessimism and his remorse, may have the right to recall that the man who of late years regrets the health and strength spent in the Imperial harness, also uttered this proud and selfish maxim:

"Fools pretend that they learn only by their own experience. I have learned by the experience of others."

We, alas! have been among those to suffer that he might gain experience in this vicarious manner. Yet we would not be unjust; we willingly admit that as, in annexing Alsace-Lorraine it was not precisely with a view to the happiness of that province, as he facetiously declared in the *Reichstag*, so was it not for his personal happiness that he undertook the unification of Germany.

The accomplishment of this task, which constitutes his sole claim upon posterity, was his personal achievement, but the idea of it, it is said, did not originate with him. He borrowed it from the Liberal party, adapting to it his individual policy of repression and absolutism. "The Germans," he said, "are worth nothing except when united by strength or by love"; and he promptly fanned into a flame racial antagonisms—for the ultimate good of the Prussian monarchy; which, for this reason, will crumble away when the Germans, having recovered their senses, shall cease to hate their neighbours.

The unity of the German nation will continue because it is adequate to the laws of human evolution, which is more and more tending to the establishment of the ethnical unification of peoples and nations in order that they may be preserved from the fancies of sovereigns and diplomats; which is tending to the destruction even of international dissemblances. The Bismarckian policy of unification succeeded because its purpose conformed to the laws of nature while upholding obsolete principles of authority which the next social revolution in Germany will destroy. William II. has done right, then, to follow in the powerful wake of the "dismissed pilot"; yet this tardy turn of the helm will save neither the futile Prussian hegemony nor the dynasty which it has founded, from the shipwreck which History reserves for the last representative of "the divine right of kings."

As a matter of fact, whether or not the followers of Bismarck will have it so, the logical end of the national evolution of Germany is a federal Republic composed of all the countries speaking the German tongue, including Austria and a part of Switzerland. This Republic will spring of itself from the fruitful soil of democratic Germany when the party of *Sozial-Democratie* shall have overcome the supreme effort against the universal affranchisement of mankind by the feudal party on the one side and the Roman Catholic on the other. These things are bound to be, whatever to the contrary Herr Otto Mittelstädt may have said in his recent pamphlet entitled "*Vor der Fluth.*"

Later, much later, when the superior principle of internationalism, repudiating all others except the principles of civilization, shall have triumphed over the artificial principle of nationalities, formerly invoked for or against peace by the oppressors of all parties, perhaps there will be but one European nation in which the peoples shall be grouped hypostatically; that is, international parties will succeed to the political alliances of to-day.

Bismarck represented will, not soul; reason, not art; statesmanship, not human impulse. Physically as well as morally his gigantic physiognomy has developed at the expense of others; even his estate of Friedrichsruh and his title of Duke of Lauenburg are—borrowed—from the Danish.

The eclecticism of means is naturally followed by variability of action, lack of logic, inconsistency of reasoning. Never has he been able to think one day as he thought the day before. One of his principles is that a man who never changes is ridiculous, and he prides himself upon his inconsistency as others do upon their constancy. "There are many people," he once said in the *Reichstag*, "who all their lives have had but one idea, to which they have always held. I am not one of that kind; I am learning every day. It is possible that in another year or some years hence, if I

Dialogue of the Dead.

A kind of Tartufe!—
Bismarck and Napoleon.

be still alive, I shall consider untenable the views which I now hold and defend." This, however, was but a repetition of the profession of faith which he made before Jules Favre on the evening of the signing of the capitulation of Paris. "To be too logical in politics is frequently a fault which leads to obstinacy. It is necessary to veer with the course of events, with the state of things, with various possibilities; to regulate one's conduct by circumstances and not by a personal opinion which is frequently a prejudice."

This humorist might perhaps have interested future generations, but he voluntarily sacrificed his vocation to politics, his success in which was too rapid and brilliant to be transformed into lasting glory. In our day, in fact, brilliant success dies with those who have attained it, and oblivion the earlier enwraps those who have abused their popularity. All is ended with the fine funeral, pompous discourses, necrological reports; then, the last candle snuffed out, the last clod of earth fallen upon the casket, there is a flight, a dispersion, a rush toward some new idol of the hour.

A German journal relates that a year ago an under-officer in Prussia, charged with the general instruction of the recruits, asked each conscript the same question: "Who is Bismarck?" Of twenty-five men, six had never heard of him, or had thought him dead, or supposed he was a French general. Such is fame in our day. This fact, however, will not prevent Bismarck's death from being copiously noticed by the French press. Yet, I repeat, I have no faith in the posthumous glory of Bismarck; he has been too great a man for his contemporaries. Too many statues have been erected in his lifetime for posterity to think of consecrating to his memory a more enduring monument. Indeed, the hour is at hand when no more monuments will be erected; when fame will join other defunct superstitions and all the ancient myths be abolished by the modern scientific movement; when, in the short time which Nature assigns to them on earth, the living will have the courage to separate from the dead, or there will be neither posterity nor nihility for anyone in the relative eternity of universal life.

THE END.

www.ingramcontent.com/pod-product-compliance
Lightning Source LLC
Chambersburg PA
CBHW020811230426
43666CB00007B/967